Veneklasen Brick

Veneklasen Brick

A Family, a Company, and a Unique
Nineteenth-Century Dutch Architectural
Movement in Michigan

Michael J. Douma

WILLIAM B. EERDMANS PUBLISHING COMPANY
GRAND RAPIDS, MICHIGAN / CAMBRIDGE, U.K.

*This book is dedicated to a
West Michigan bricklayer, my grandfather,
Peter Douma (1922 – 2005)*

Wm. B. Eerdmans Publishing Co.
255 Jefferson Ave. S.E., Grand Rapids, Michigan 49503 /
P.O. Box 163, Cambridge CB3 9PU U.K.

Printed in the United States of America

10 09 08 07 06 05   7 6 5 4 3 2 1

ISBN 0-8028-3163-X

www.eerdmans.com

In Remembrance of
Betty Shoemaker
Photo Archivist and Librarian

With affectionate memories
of many years as a friend and a member
of the Zeeland Historical Society

Contents

Contents

Preface

This work began in the spring of 2004, when I approached Geoffrey Reynolds of the Joint Archives of Holland with ideas for a summer project. During the past year I had witnessed the destruction of a Veneklasen house at 10715 Paw Paw Drive in Holland Township. On a run out of town I was saddened to see a quaint red brick house with brown horses roaming a large, fenced-in backyard bulldozed to make way for the new headquarters of Macatawa Bank. Frustrated that we, the Joint Archives, as a local history depository, had heard nothing of the impending destruction of a local nineteenth-century home, I searched for information on other local brick houses. To my dismay, I found but a few scant articles and some notable but largely unfinished research on the subject. With approval, I began my own research, which combined archival digging and an extensive field survey. After four months of research and writing the results are now before you.

A certain Hope College history professor once told me that the preface is where you thank everyone that you've ever known in your entire life. I will attempt to keep this list of gratitudes to a minimum, all the while hoping that no one has been forgotten. First of all, thanks to the Joint Archives of Holland (Geoffrey Reynolds and Lori Trethewey) for sponsoring and supporting this project, and for all the opportunities and friendship of the last four years. Due credit is given to Elton Bruins of the Van Raalte Institute, who initiated the Oral History Project in 1977, for his help and continued support. There is no more devoted historian of Holland, Michigan. I am thankful to the Veneklasen descendants who aided me with their family history. The contributions of a few, I must note, were exceptionally helpful, including those of Howard Veneklasen Jr., Leslie Lampen, and Elaine Van Zoeren. May this work be a tribute to your (quite large and extended) family. Thanks to all the homeowners who were welcoming participants in the house survey, for your willingness to open your doors and share photographs and stories. Institutions that were helpful in creating this work included the Holland Museum, Byron Center Historical Society, Heritage Hall at Calvin College, the Grand Rapids Public Archives, Bernard Historical Museum, Allegan County Historical Society, and especially the Zeeland Historical Society through Kit Karsten and Chris Pennings. In regards to material about Hamilton, I thank Ruth Tidd and for help with Cloverdale history and an afternoon tour of the township I thank George Leonard. I must also mention the work of Matt Van Dyken, GPS Programmer for the City of Holland, who is responsible for creating a brilliant map of local brick houses.

Through these persons and institutions I have discovered a great wealth of information. My one regret is that I have been unable to find any business records from the Veneklasen brickyards. Probably they were destroyed years ago. A list of business transactions of Veneklasen & Co., even if it covered only a single year, would be a treasure. All photographs that have no citation are property of the Joint Archives of Holland. All translations from Dutch to English are my own, unless otherwise noted.

2004   *Michael Douma*

Introduction and Historiography

This book began as a project whose goal was to document the history of Dutch brick houses in and around Holland, Michigan. Such a history, however, would be impossible without much information on the Veneklasen brickyards and the family who operated them. In addition, the brickworkers and builders of the houses deserve mention and a chapter is devoted to them. Furthermore, this work seeks to show similarities and contrasts between West Michigan Dutch vernacular architecture and its Netherlandic antecedent. Last, but not least, the author is concerned with the conservation and preservation of local brick houses. Related to this concern is a new (2004) and extensive survey of relevant existing and destroyed houses.

Veneklasen houses represent a significant and unique architectural and historical development. They are stylistically interesting in that they mix local materials, Dutch craftsmanship, and broad trends in American nineteenth-century architecture. While no complete survey has heretofore been accomplished, I am by no means the first to have attempted to document the history of Veneklasen houses.

In 1975, Don Marek, a graduate student under the supervision of Dr. Henry Glassie of the Folklore Institute at the University of Indiana, undertook a summer project to document Veneklasen brick houses. Marek's research was productive but short-lived, as he had the time and energy to research only about thirty houses, nearly all of which were located in Zeeland and nearby Borculo, Michigan. He took photographs of the houses and interviewed their owners, but did little archival research, and some of his conclusions appear premature and unsubstantiated. For instance, he claims that "since the early settlers were inexperienced in building with timber and many were experienced and talented masons, they soon began to build with Veneklasen brick."[1] The result of Marek's labor was a general interest article that appeared in a 1975 edition of the *Wonderland Magazine* of the *Grand Rapids Press*. When handing over his notes to the Zeeland Historical Society, he noted his hope that someone would finish the research by documenting all the houses that he had missed.

Cecilia Ver Hage, utilizing the information gathered by Marek, assembled for the Zeeland Historical Society a booklet that was printed in 1986. She presented photographs and short histories of about two dozen Veneklasen brick houses in and around Zeeland. She also added a short sketch of the history of the Veneklasen brickyard, attaching copies of some relevant primary source documents. The major strength of Ver Hage's work is the individual stories of the houses; her weaknesses include guesswork on dating the houses and a lack of citations.

While Ver Hage was busy compiling her booklet (which is still used at the Zeeland Museum), Fred Van Hartesveldt, a local high school history teacher, had also begun research on Veneklasen houses. Van Hartesveldt located nearly one hundred Veneklasen houses and noted their architectural characteristics. But although his survey was large, it was by no means complete. In a 1987 article for *Michigan History* magazine, Van Hartesveldt drew from Ver Hage's work to pen a brief history of brickworkers in the area. The main fo-

---

1. Don Marek's Project, 1975, page 2. Available at Zeeland Museum.

cus of his research was the unique decorative brickwork of the houses. Van Hartesveldt's work, however important for its insights into decorative architecture, creates more questions than it answers because his research, like Marek's, is sprinkled with speculation and lacks background.

Van Hartesveldt was largely copied by Holland resident Randy Vande Water for an article that appeared in identical form in both *Origins* magazine of Calvin College and the *Holland Historical Trust Review* of the Holland Museum in 1991. Vande Water extracted more information from Ver Hage's work in the form of a chart of the brick production of Veneklasen & Co. throughout its years of operation. This chart relies entirely on a single article printed in the *Ottawa County Times* in 1892. Although his work offered no new viewpoints, Vande Water did contribute some information about the Veneklasen family, which had been absent in previous works.

In 1995 two short articles advocating preservation of the houses appeared in the *Holland Sentinel*. These were penned, respectively, by Larry Wagenaar, then director of the Joint Archives of Holland, and Ann Kiewel, serving as director of the Holland Historical Trust. Although Wagenaar and Kiewel did no research into the houses, they once again brought the houses to the public eye.

More recently, in 1998 Janna (Baron) Bailey researched Veneklasen houses for her master's thesis in historic preservation at Eastern Michigan University. This thesis relied heavily on secondary sources, particularly the works of Marek and Van Hartesveldt. Bailey, however, offered further interpretations and insights about the movement to build brick houses. She writes that the Veneklasen family did not specifically promote the building style, as earlier researchers had suggested. Bailey's interpretation is based on the claim that the local brick house movement, and patterned brickwork in particular, had been long underway when the Veneklasen family house was built in 1873.[2] My re-

---

2. Janna (Baron) Bailey, Unpublished Master's Thesis on Polychromatic Brick Buildings in Ottawa, Allegan, and Kent Counties. (Eastern Michigan University, 1998), 10-11.

search will contest this, showing that the Veneklasen family played some role in the spread of the designs on the houses which now bear the family name. Bailey also supports the idea that wealth — new wealth in particular — was a reason why certain families built brick houses. While a keen observation overlooked by other recent researchers, this was not novel, as it was already well supported by the historian Jacob Van Hinte in 1928.[3] The most important contribution of Bailey's work is in suggesting ideas for preservation. These ideas include (1) the creation of a self-guided driving tour pamphlet (2) the formation of a preservation organization and (3) the development of a Veneklasen house into a museum.

Clearly, then, there has been persistent interest in the research and preservation of Veneklasen houses. All of the listed researchers were well aware of the daunting task that a comprehensive survey would pose. Yet in the end they all believed that such a survey should be conducted. The complete results of this survey, including files for many Veneklasen brick houses and buildings, can be found at the Joint Archives of Holland. This collection is an excellent resource for those who would like to restore a Veneklasen home or learn more about the Veneklasen family or brickyards.

---

3. Jacob Van Hinte, *Netherlands in America,* trans. Adriaan de Wit and ed. Robert P. Swierenga (Grand Rapids: Baker Book House, 1928, repr. 1985), 336-338.

Part I

A History of Veneklasen Brick

Chapter 1

Early Houses in the *Kolonie* and Demand for Brick

When the first Dutch settlers arrived on the shores of Lake Macatawa in 1847, there was little by way of shelter to welcome and protect them. A contingent of men, among them the respected leader Albertus Van Raalte, arrived first. After trekking from Allegan through the wilderness, this group of men lodged at the shanty of Isaac Fairbanks and the neighboring Old Wing Mission of George Smith, on section three of Fillmore Township. Smith, a missionary to the Indians, and Fairbanks, his government-appointed agriculture aide, introduced the men to the area. Soon, inspired by a rousing speech from Van Raalte, they began to build log houses in preparation for the arrival of their fellow Dutch settlers. But building log houses proved troublesome, as the Dutch were inexperienced at felling trees and lacked proper cutting tools. When the rest of the settlers arrived there was a housing shortage, so that many constructed makeshift lean-tos from hemlock branches, tucking away their large wooden chests, filled to the brim with their possessions from the old country.[1]

1. "Egbert Fredericks' Pioneer Memories," in Henry S. Lucas, *Dutch Immi-*

Early local house
Courtesy Zeeland
Historical Society

To say that there were no buildings in the area before the arrival of the Dutch would be misleading, but such buildings were few and far between. At Point Superior, now Waukazoo Woods, there stood a sawmill and a few houses. Further north, at Port Sheldon, a new village was sprouting up around a hotel serving travelers on Lake Michigan. The Indians native to the region also had a few log houses, but lived for the most part in tents. At the Indian village on the south shore of Lake Macatawa, there was even a relatively large wood frame building, which was used for meetings when a Catholic priest visited.[2]

The earliest houses of the Dutch in the Holland area were also built of logs or wooden beams and often covered with bark or pine shingles. For permanent dwellings, however, brick foundations were needed. Brick would have also been in high demand for building

grant *Memoirs and Related Writings*. (Grand Rapids: William B. Eerdmans Publishing Company, 1955, repr. 1997), i:55-72.

2. "Isaac Fairbanks' Recollections," in Lucas, *Dutch Immigrant Memoirs and Related Writings*, i:377-82.

chimneys and well-casings. Yet importing bricks to Holland in the first years of settlement would have been difficult. There were few roads leading in or out of the city, and of those roads, not many were large enough or safe enough for oxen-drawn wagons. Sailing ships on Lake Michigan, by and large, would have been too insignificant and unreliable to carry enough bricks to make the trade profitable. Even if bricks could have been transported by ship, the channel between Lake Michigan and Lake Macatawa did not open until 1858. Prior to this, all goods imported by ship had to be unloaded at the pier on Lake Michigan and transferred to smaller boats, which would then cross Lake Macatawa to supply the city. Of course, when enough ice formed on Lake Michigan in the winter, this shipping trade ground to a halt. Winter sledding through the woods to Allegan and elsewhere provided Holland with necessities. In short, the town needed a local brickmaker, at least until the lanes of transport could supply bricks from the outside.

Enter Jan Hendrik Veneklasen, a skilled brickmaker who emigrated from the Netherlands in 1847 and must have been aware of this need for brick. Of course, as a settler in the West Michigan wilderness, his primary objective was most likely to clear land to plant crops and provide for his wife and eight children. For Jan and the Dutch settlers all around, it would prove to be a difficult first year. Tragedy struck the Veneklasen family when Jan's wife, Aaltje (Alice), died on August 12, 1847. She was perhaps a victim of malaria, which thrived thanks to the local proliferation of swampland and the lack of available medicine. Disease was hardly the only worry, though. West Michigan was in these days still a wild land with wolves and bears, and relations with the Indians were never easy. In this environment the concern of the settlers turned to creating tillable land, which was all too rare amidst the thick forests. Laborers were called upon to clear the forests.

Despite this call for labor, Jan Veneklasen's son, Berend J., left home and went to work for a brickyard in the city of Allegan. As the eldest son (he turned nineteen in 1847), Berend was probably sent out to earn money, as hard currency was difficult to come by in the

Kolonie. Berend returned within the year, and having witnessed the profitability of the brick industry, he may have urged his father to divert some time and resources away from agriculture and back to brickmaking, the trade he knew best. Thus in 1848, Jan Veneklasen and his son Berend opened a brickyard on section seventeen of Holland Township. The first clay pits were located on the north side of Sixteenth Street, across from what became the property of Ben Van Raalte (Van Raalte Farm). By 1853 they completed a move to a location just north of the present Groningen Cemetery. In 1872, a more favorable location was found on the west end of Zeeland. Indeed, the yard continued to move around the Groningen area, exhausting one clay pit after another. Known by various names, all of which included 'Veneklasen', it was the first brick company in the Holland area, and would prove to be the most successful and longest lasting.[3]

In its earliest years, this brick business was small and local. In 1850, Jan and Berend Veneklasen managed to produce around fifty thousand bricks. For the Holland fifty-year celebration in 1897, area resident Reijer van Zwaluwenburg recalled,

> A little beyond the bridge by the present Groningen cemetery we saw father [Jan Hendrik] and his son Berend Jan in overalls which had been rolled up above their knees. They stood plying their shovels and working the clay with their hands and feet.[4]

These first bricks probably went to make chimneys, as few settlers yet had the wealth to afford brick houses. One exception was Andries Steketee, who in 1851 was credited with having the first brick

3. The efforts at the first site were short-lived, and the site in Groningen was begun by 1853, perhaps as early as 1851. The Zeeland site was chosen by 1872, but clay pits in the Groningen area remained active.

4. Translation of *"Een weinig over de brug van het nu oude Groninger kerkhof, zagen wij vader Veneklaasen met zijn zoon, de blauwe overalls oprold tot over de knieen. Zij stonden in de klei met een schop in de hand en als het ware met handen en voeten de klei bewerkende om er steen van te bakken."* From "Reijer Van Zwaluwenberg's Life Sketch," in Lucas, *Dutch Immigrant Memoirs,* i. 421.

Steketee / Scholten house at 1811 112th Ave. 1995 photo
Courtesy Elton Bruins

house in the colony.[5] The exclusively red brick Steketee House was built within a mile of the Veneklasen brickyard.[6] The house was stra-

5. *Sheboygan Nieuws Bode,* 26 September 1851. The author was surprised and excited to see a brick house being built. It was *"iets extra"* (something special). This house was probably made from brick procured from the very first clay pit in Holland Township.

6. Steketee began a business of selling staves, which were shipped on flatboats down the Black River. He is also credited with having built the first boat in the colony. Early settler Abraham Stegeman claims that Steketee sold this business in 1857 to Hendrik Scholten, who then built a spacious brick house near "Scholten's Bridge" (Lucas, *Dutch Immigrant Memoirs,* i. 163). This, however, must be incorrect. According to the land deed, Steketee sold this property and house to Rykelt Scholten on July 5, 1855. The Steketee House then became the Scholten House. Steketee and his two sons died in a shipwreck near St. Joseph, Michigan, in 1857. See also *Holland City News,* 3 March 1930.

7

Veneklasen
advertisement in
de Verzamelaar, 10
September 1862

BEKENDMAKING.

De ondergeteekende maakt bij dezen be-
kend, dat hij eenen oven met **baksteenen**
klaar heeft, die voor vervoer gereed zijn.
Allen, die Baksteenen noodig hebben, kun-
nen dezelve verkrijgen aan de

STEENBAKKERIJ

van BEREND JAN VEENEKLAZEN

te GRONINGEN.

Berend J. Veeneklazen.

Holland, Mich., 15 Aug , 1862.

tegically situated near a bridge on the banks of the Black River and
was just a short walk from where settlers hoped to build a prosper-
ous town called Groningen.[7] In 1853, another report of activity in
building brick houses surfaced. *De Hollander,* a Dutch-English bilin-
gual newspaper in Holland, reported "Today people are busy with
bringing together the materials for the second brick house in Holland. These bricks are being transported and baked by our friend
J. H. Veenenklaasen [sic] nearby Groningen."[8] It is not known
whether the writer considered the Steketee House, which officially
stood outside Holland's boundaries, or another brick house, to be
Holland's first. In Holland today, no brick houses from the 1850s remain standing.

7. The Groningen settlement failed in favor of Zeeland and Holland. Also see
Lucas, *Dutch Immigrant Memoirs,* i 135. Jan Hendriks Stegink mentions that in
1848 there were about thirty houses in Groningen, and all but two were log houses.
The other two were probably wood frame houses.

8. Translation of *"Men is hier thans bezig met de bouwstoffen, bijeen te
brengen, voor het tweede steene huis in Town Holland. Deze steenen worden
vervaardigd en gebakken door onzen vriend J. H. Veenenklaasen, nabij
Groningen."* In *De Hollander,* 21 September, 1853.

Van Vleck Hall, circa 1890

Brick houses, rare in the Holland area in the 1850s gradually became more common throughout the 1860s as the Veneklasen brickyard grew. In 1862, Berend Veneklasen advertised in *De Verzamelaar*, a local Dutch-language religious newspaper. His advertisement, printed in four consecutive weekly issues in September, illustrates that his was still a little-known company. In fact, the title of his advertisement was "Making Acquaintance." In full, the translation reads,

> With this, the undersigned makes it known that he has a kiln with bricks that are ready for transport. Everyone who needs bricks can get them at the brickyard of Berend Jan Veeneklazen [sic] in Groningen.[9]

9. *De Verzamelaar*, 10 September 1862.

9

It is noteworthy that, while the nineteenth century Dutch were lenient in spelling last names, the use of a 'z' in 'Veeneklazen' is peculiar. It probably reflects the American English pronunciation of the word.[10]

An example of early Veneklasen brick can be seen in Holland, where the oldest remaining brick structure is an academic building, Van Vleck Hall. Built in 1857 on the grounds of the Holland Academy (what would become Hope College) Van Vleck was, at the time of its construction, the largest brick building in the area. It became the centerpiece of an institution, used in nearly every facet of academic life.[11] In its English-language section, *De Hollander* reported in flowing language about the modesty shown at such an historical event,

> There was . . . no burying of leaden boxes filled with parchments and papers and other historical debris of still more leaden dullness than the saturnine casket in which they were concealed. All was most enimently [sic] practical, and devoid of pretence, and would have particularly pleased Mr. Bounderby, had he been present. — There was no flighty nonsense about the sturdy mason, who wielded a genuine trowl [sic] and wore a real toil worn apron, and handled the boulders without mittens with a plain homely purpose, which was, merely to build up his wall as fast as possible. . . .[12]

10. In Dutch, the name 'Veeneklaasen' might mean that the family was of a class *(klas)* of people who lived or worked near peat bogs (sing. *veen,* plural *venen*). Peat bogs are fairly common in the northeastern provinces of the Netherlands. One might speculate that a tradition of working the soil, for peat or clay, passed through generations.

11. As teenagers all six children of Roloef Veneklasen attended the Preparatory School at Hope College and would have been familiar with Van Vleck Hall. Some of them also attended college at Hope. See JAH Collection H88-0255, Student Index of Names.

12. *De Hollander,* 20 May 1857.

The bricks of Van Vleck tell us much about the history of the early brickmaking industry.[13] First of all, the bricks are not completely uniform in shape. Local brickmakers did not yet have the ability (read machinery) to produce solid color, uniformly-cut bricks. These early bricks vary in color from maroon to red and from orange to white. This range on the color spectrum represents the heterogeneous nature of the clay as well as the placement of bricks in the kiln, darker bricks being those which were baked longer or at higher temperatures. The laying of brick on Van Vleck and other early Veneklasen buildings is also peculiar. In 1882, a visitor to the area from the Netherlands described this technique. "In America they lay bricks from the inside of the wall so one seldom sees a ladder outside the building. They lay the brick six courses upon another with a top course between."[14] A top course is a layer in which the bricks have been turned so that their short end sides are visible to the outside. This pattern was still in use in the 20th century.

In the 1860s brick houses were being built in increasing numbers. But why, surrounded by suitable timber, did the Dutch immigrants build houses out of brick at all? Chances are that most had lived in brick houses in the Netherlands and they simply thought of brick as a more suitable material for houses. Don Marek, who researched Veneklasen houses in the 1970s, thought that the group of Dutch immigrants included many skilled masons from the Netherlands who naturally applied their knowledge to build from brick instead of wood. But wood always remained the primary building material. While there were enough masons and brickworkers to promote a flourishing brick industry, there was an even larger number of carpenters. In a 1987 article, Van Hartesveldt elaborates on the numerical supremacy of Dutch carpenters when he writes, "Thirty-nine brickmasons and 273 carpenters lived in the northern row of town-

13. Another early (c. 1860s) Veneklasen building on Hope's campus was the "De Hope" printing office located on Columbia between 10th and 11th Streets.

14. Johannes Van Dyk, quoted from 1881 in "The Holland Kolonie," *Origins* 1, Number 2 (1983), 3-8.

ships in Allegan County and the southern row of Ottawa County from 1850 to 1880. Almost all emigrated from the Netherlands."[15] Yet perhaps there were more men involved in the brick industry that the census relates. For instance, only the lead mason would call himself a mason, while other brickworkers and brickmakers would simply be recorded as "day laborers." Conversely, carpenters included not only those who worked on houses, but also ship carpenters employed in Holland's extensive boat building industry. In the 1860 census, even Berend J. Veneklasen, at 31 years of age and co-owner of a brickyard, was not listed as a brickmaker, but as a farmer, with an estate value of a thousand dollars and a personal wealth of two hundred.[16] It wasn't necessarily a few skilled masons who built brick houses, but many laborers who worked part time, seasonally, and temporarily, at the brickyards and at the worksites. Some of these workers were skilled carpenters but many more may have been farmers seeking part-time employment.

Skilled masons, however, are responsible for the most distinctive feature of Veneklasen houses, namely their decorative patterned brickwork. These masons worked independently from the brickyards and had the ability to experiment with new patterns and styles. With no two houses having the same patterns, the masons left a unique legacy with their artwork. The country of origin for the vast majority of local brick workers was the Netherlands, and it is from the Netherlands that they brought a tradition of decorative brick-work.

Building with brick has a long history in the Netherlands. The low-lying country has significant clay regions. Brickmaking was learned from the Romans and became more common in the Late Middle Ages; many brick churches from the thirteenth century remain in the Netherlands to this day. By the sixteenth century the use

15. Fred Van Hartesveldt, "Decorative Brick: A Gift to Michigan From the Dutch," *Michigan History,* May/June 1987, 37. See also JAH Pamphlet File, City of Holland, Historical and Architectural Reconnaissance Level Survey, July 1988.

16. 1860 Ottawa County Census, p. 488.

**1882 white and red patterned brick schoolhouse
in Groningen, Michigan. Photo circa 1925**
Courtesy of Zeeland Historical Society

of brick was widespread and common for houses as well as for public buildings. Wood housing became less common as the forests of Europe gave way to growing populations. Other building material included stone, which was used for decoration on only the most lavish brick buildings. Here an architectural style of red brick contrasting with white stone was popular. According to architectural historians Campbell and Price, "The facades of the wealthy were bichromatic, the white decorative elements standing out against a darker background."[17] White and red patterned brick houses in the

17. James Campbell and Will Pryce, *Brick: A World History* (London, Thames and Hudson, 2003), 165.

Netherlands may then trace their lineage to this white stone/red brick phenomenon.

In the seventeenth century, Northern European immigrants to America brought with them the skills to continue the decorative brickwork tradition. The most prolific and famous American brickwork from that century and the next can be found in New York and Pennsylvania, and was created by, respectively, the Dutch and Pennsylvania Dutch (Germans). Later, in the nineteenth century, the Dutch immigrants to Michigan brought with them the same brickwork knowledge. Using red brick from the Groningen yard (and also, later, the Hamilton yard) in contrast with white brick from the Zeeland yard, masons created recognizable patterns that were highly imitated. It is possible that patterned brickwork was first used locally in the 1850s or early 1860s, but no existing examples have been confirmed.[18] The search has also been hindered by inaccurate information about this early, less documented period. For example, a booklet entitled "Sites of Dutch Influence in Western Michigan" published in 1996 by the Dutch-American Historical Commission indicates that the Groningen schoolhouse at 10753 Paw Paw Drive was built in 1855. This date *would* make it the first Veneklasen structure with patterned brickwork. However, this schoolhouse was actually built in 1881, replacing an earlier wood frame school.[19] At least three Veneklasen houses in Groningen date to the 1850s, but to claim the elusive title of "first polychromatic (multi-colored) Veneklasen brick structure," it must be shown that the brickwork was completed at or near the same date as the house. An example of a red herring is the polychromatic house which stood at 10715 Paw Paw Dr. until its destruction in 2002, and which dates to 1857. This would make it the oldest of its kind. Yet it is possible, even likely, that the patterned brickwork on this house was done during a later edition to the

18. One notable red herring is the red and white patterned brickwork Peachbelt schoolhouse in Ganges Township, which was built in 1867 but whose brick veneer dates to 1898 or 1899.

19. Holland *Evening Sentinel,* 20 August 1936.

house, not as an original feature. Such is the case with a nearby house at 11045 Paw Paw Drive, which has an original portion dating to 1859 and a much larger patterned brickwork addition from 1885.

In the 1870s in West Michigan, patterned brickwork as an art style was revived and its use became widespread. Its popularity can mostly be attributed to the availability of relatively inexpensive brick and the desire to build distinctive and attractive homes. It also seems that the Veneklasen family played some role in the proliferation of the style. Building their own homes out of the company's brick was not only economical and practical for the Veneklasen clan, but may have served as an advertisement to other prospective homebuilders. The Berend J. Veneklasen family home, situated on a hill overlooking the west end of Zeeland, Michigan, was built in 1873, in the early stages of the use of polychromatic brickwork in the area. Bailey, we

10715 Paw Paw Drive. Destroyed 2002
Photo courtesy of Elton Bruins

Berend J. Veneklasen home, 10823 Chicago Drive

recall, claimed that the Veneklasen family was not responsible for promoting the style because their house was built too late to be considered a model for others.[20] But a new survey shows that few, if any, houses with patterned brickwork predate this house. In 1872, the Veneklasens opened new clay pits on the west end of Zeeland, moved their kilns nearby, and built a factory. With this new source of clay in Zeeland, they began to make white brick in addition to red. With these two colors local masons were now able to create patterned brickwork motifs for the first time. The Veneklasens wholeheartedly accepted this trend and understood the benefits that it would bring to their business. As soon as they could afford to do so, they built brick houses on their own property. Most of these houses exhibited patterned brickwork.

20. Janna (Baron) Bailey, Unpublished Master's Thesis on Polychromatic Brick Buildings in Ottawa, Allegan, and Kent Counties. (East Michigan University, 1998), 10-11.

Howard Veneklasen Jr.
of Holland, Michigan,
with Hendrik
Veneklasen of the
Netherlands at the
Veneklasen family
home in Holten,
Overijssel, the
Netherlands, 1994

The role of the Veneklasen family in the promotion of patterned brickwork may go deeper yet. In 1975 Marek claimed that "the brick-work has roots in the Dutch brick building tradition, but no exact antecedent has been found there [in the Netherlands]."[21] My research has led to what just might be the antecedent of all Veneklasen homes in West Michigan: the home of Jan Hendrik Veneklasen himself. Jan left his home village in the Netherlands at an early age to work as an apprentice at a brickyard in a neighboring town. For nearly thirty years prior to emigrating to America, he was involved in that industry, and would have been well acquainted with brick

21. Don Marek's Project, 1975, page 2. Available at Zeeland Museum.

house architecture. Jan's house, located by descendant Howard Veneklasen Jr. in a 1994 trip to the Netherlands, bears remarkable similarities in brickwork to that of the brick houses scattered across West Michigan. Could it be that Jan, or his son Berend J., was primarily responsible for influencing local builders to build in this style? The enigma is intriguing. If it were not a Veneklasen specifically who was responsible for this movement, it may have been a number of other emigrants from the same area in the Netherlands who wished to replicate the familiar motifs of home. The contrasting red and white brick pattern is not ubiquitous in the Netherlands and may be specific to a certain region, including the provinces of Overijssel, Drenthe, and Groningen. Dutch historian Annemieke Galema, writes, "Presumably these houses were built by masons from Groningen [Netherlands], because one can also come across this sort of architecture in the province of Groningen."[22]

22. Translation of, "*Vermoedlijk zijn deze huizen gebouwd door Groningse metselaars, omdat men dit soort architectuur ook in de provincie Groningen aantreft*" from Annemieke Galema, *Van de Ene en de Andere Kant* (Rijksuniversiteit Groningen, 1993), 108-09.

Chapter 2

Fire and a Building Boom (1870-1900)

In 1871 a great fire devastated the city of Holland, burning to the ground nearly two thirds of its buildings. It is not known exactly how many Veneklasen houses came down as a result. In his inventory of the destruction, Holland's first historian and a witness to the fire, Gerrit van Schelven, writes of three lost brick houses, but he mentions that his list is by no means complete.[1] In downtown Holland, only two brick houses have survived both the fire and the ravages of time. These two houses, the 1868 Coatsworth House at 236 West 9th Street and an 1870 house at 238 Washington Avenue, belong to small residential pocket that was miraculously spared by the fire.

Determined to rise up from the ashes, Hollanders set to rebuilding. In the wake of the fire, and due to a rapidly expanding population in the area, timbered land was at a premium. In the spring of

---

1. "A Contemporary Account of the Holland Fire," by Gerrit van Schelven, 187, in Lucas, *Dutch Immigrant Memoirs*, ii.7-13. The three brick houses van Schelven mentions are (1) the brick house of T. W. Berkompas on the north side of 7th Street; (2) the large and attractive house of C. deJong; and (3) the new brick house of P. Winter.

5736 140th Street in Fillmore Township
Courtesy Eileen and Russell Sandy

1876, the *Holland City News* noted that lumber was becoming scarce. The paper claimed that brick would replace wood as the primary building material.[2] This was already the case downtown on Eighth Street, where brick was being used almost exclusively in the construction of new stores and various other businesses. The fire and the destruction it had left behind changed some minds about building in wood, but the fire had also financially ruined many of Holland's citizens and, for the time being, few could spare the expense required to build a brick house. Thus there is a noteworthy absence

2. *Holland City News*, 13 May 1876.

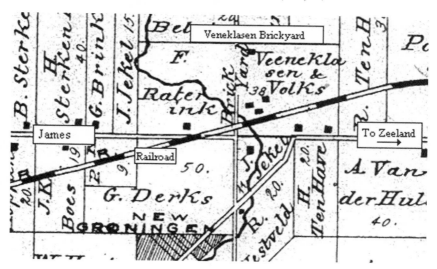

Map of brickyard area in Zeeland, 1876 atlas of Ottawa County

of brick houses in Holland from the 1870s. Elsewhere, however, in the small villages outside of the city, building with brick became increasingly popular. Everything seemed to come together to make brick housing affordable. Wages and materials were cheap, and insurance rates for houses were dropping.[3] This favorable trend continued, and it was noted in 1879 that "it may be many years before labor and material will be as cheap again as it is at present."[4] The housing market was experiencing a boom which lasted from the 1870s throughout the 1880s as the population of West Michigan, fueled by regular immigration to the area, continued to grow.

In the 1870s, polychromatic brickwork houses also grew in popularity. For the most part, Veneklasen brick was sent to Dutch clients, but outside of the Dutch communities others must have taken note of the style as well. Already in 1874, a red and white Veneklasen brick grange hall had been built in Georgetown Township. Veneklasen

3. *Holland City News*, 17 June 1876.
4. *Holland City News*, 2 January 1879.

brick was in high demand, and the season's surplus often sold out. A project begun one year might have to wait for the next to buy the extra needed bricks. This may have been the case with the house at 5736 140th Street in Fillmore Township. This unique house has one section built in white brick with red decoration, and a second section with primarily red brick and white embellishments. It is possible that the workers began building the house with white brick but during the second year of construction were only able to purchase red brick.

While brickmakers profited from demand from the local housing sector, perhaps the most important development for the area brick industry in the early 1870s was the introduction of the railroad. A sidetrack of the Chicago and West Michigan Railroad fed into the Zeeland brickyard, where bricks could be loaded directly onto the rail cars. In 1878, nearly three quarters of the Veneklasen brick production was shipped by rail, and in 1880 the company's exports amounted to two hundred railcar loads.[5] This improvement in transportation was revolutionary. The railroad could not only transport more brick than could oxen-pulled carts, but it could ship it further, therefore expanding the market for Veneklasen brick. Now bricks were shipped east to Grand Rapids, as far north as Traverse City and south to Chicago.[6] Too, Veneklasen & Co. was now able to supply brick for larger orders. In 1878, for example, they had a single contract for 900,000 bricks.[7] An 1876 atlas map shows the railroad cutting through the Veneklasen property (on it, the name 'Bolks' is misspelled as 'Volks,' and houses are designated by black squares).

In the late 1860s and early 1870s there also began a movement to build schoolhouses out of brick. One report claims that Veneklasen & Co. played a role in the actual construction of a schoolhouse in Zeeland,[8] while another article tells of Veneklasen brick being used

5. *Holland City News*, 12 October 1878, and 17 January 1880.
6. *Portrait & Biographical Record of Muskegon & Ottawa Counties, Michigan.* (Chicago: Biographical Publishing, 1893), 381-82.
7. *Holland City News*, 26 July 1878.
8. *Holland City News*, 2 January 1879.

East Holland schoolhouse, circa 1890
Courtesy Zeeland Historical Society

to build a new brick school in Holland Township.[9] Not only were the builders successful in marketing these schoolhouse designs in Holland and Zeeland but also in many other places across Ottawa, Allegan, and Kent Counties. Many a village took comfort in providing its children with a warm, soundly constructed, and aesthetically pleasing place to learn. One brick schoolhouse in Overisel was proudly described as having a floor of alternating ash and walnut strips, and even a belfry with a bell.[10] Of the few schoolhouses that survive, some have been converted into houses. The East Holland schoolhouse, pictured above, sits abandoned and largely forgotten.

9. *Holland City News,* 11 February 1882.
10. *Holland City News,* 8 December 1877.

With increased demand for bricks and an extended market, other brickyard companies were formed, challenging the Veneklasens' near-monopoly. One was that of Roost and Klaasen, which was situated at the head of Lake Macatawa. This yard, which began operating in the mid-1870s, appeared to be in a prime location, as bricks could be directly loaded onto ships at the plant.[11] Roost & Co., as it came to be called, was able to produce fifteen thousand bricks per day with its new machinery. They must have conducted a substantial enterprise with some success, because Roost's business endured for at least ten years. The last newspaper mention of Roost & Co. was in 1888. The yard intended to begin that April, weather permitting.[12]

While other brickyards had limited success in selling brick for public buildings, the Veneklasen's continued to dominate the market of bricks for houses. The company also began expanding, as they purchased part of the brickyard of A. Bolks & Co. in 1877. Bolks had been a business partner of the Veneklasens as early as 1874. Why he left the company is uncertain. It wasn't that the trade was in decline. Demand for bricks remained higher than supply in the 1870s and the Veneklasens worked feverishly to increase production. Much help came with the introduction of machines at the factory. With new machinery in 1876 the company was able to make twenty thousand bricks per day.[13]

In early 1880, the Holland City *News* reported that the Veneklasen brickyard in Zeeland was going to enlarge, doubling its capacity and employing fifty workers for the next season. Later that year the company also added a new kiln. To keep their kilns operating enough to meet demand, the brickyard needed a great amount of

---

11. *Holland City News*, 16 August 1879. More specifically, this brickyard was located at 2nd Street and River Ave., near the present wastewater treatment facility.

12. *Holland City News*, 25 May 1878, 16 February 1888, and 3 November 1888. Another local brickyard at this time was that of Gerrit van den Beldt and his son-in-law John Balgooyen. This may be the same Klaasen who later operated a brickyards in Grand Rapids.

13. *Holland City News*, 31 January 1874, and 29 April 1876, and 9 June 1877.

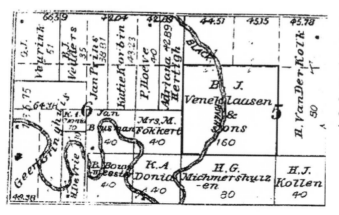

1876 atlas of Allegan County showing Veneklasen land in the northwest corner of Overisel Township

lumber. In 1878 alone, the Veneklasen brickyards consumed 1,200 cords of wood (there are 128 cubic feet in a cord). In 1880, the brickyard ran an advertisement asking for 2,000 more cords.[14] The fire of 1871 had destroyed much local forest and the cost of firewood was high. Perhaps in an attempt to find their own source of lumber, Veneklasen & Sons, as the company then hailed itself, bought a half section of timbered land in Overisel Township for $12,210 in cash.[15] The price of local wood continued to rise significantly enough that in 1889 the wood support beams for a brick house in Zeeland were shipped in from Grand Haven.[16] Later, the brickyard would switch to coal and then oil for fuel for its kilns.

In the 1880s West Michigan saw a continuation of building brick houses and a bustling economy. While the cost of brick was going down in general, brick houses remained more expensive than wood houses and were built primarily for the well-to-do.[17] An 1883 con-

14. *Holland City News,* 12 October 1878, 17 January 1880, and 3 September 1880.

15. *Holland City News,* 25 February 1882. This section of land is presently a golf course.

16. See file on house at 644 E. Lincoln. Available at JAH.

17. Brick was usually paid for in units of one thousand, and a transportation fee was often included. While I have found no early prices for Veneklasen Brick, a brickyard in a similar situation, that of Wilhelm Fleming in Sheboygan, Wisconsin,

Ocobock home at 2994 Byron Road in Jamestown Township, circa 1890
Courtesy Larry Ocobock

tract between Herman Zieleyn to build the house of Mannes
Veldhuis of Overisel, listed the total cost of the house at $360. It was
to be paid in three payments of $100, $100, and $160 dollars for three
respective stages of construction.[18] This house, which I have been
unable to locate, was probably on the low end of the price scale.
Other houses, such as the Ocobock house, pictured above, were veri-
table mansions in their day and might have cost twice that much to

sold a thousand bricks for between $3.37 and $3.75 in 1853. *Sheboygan Niewsbode,*
12 July, 1853.

18. 1883 Contract of Herman Zieleyn and Mannes Velduis in Johannes Van
Dyke, "Kolonie," 8.

Fourth of July gathering at the DePree home in Zeeland, Michigan, 1894
Courtesy Zeeland Historical Society

build. In 1887, one thousand Veneklasen bricks went for a little over six dollars, roughly a working man's weekly wages.[19] This cost limited potential customers. The DePree home, pictured above, is another example of a brick house dating to the 1880's that belonged to a relatively wealthy family. Flags have been brought out for celebrating the Fourth of July. The family is well dressed and owns luxury items like a bicycle and baby carriage. (Notice also that the children in the front row are brandishing toy pistols.)

From 1890 to 1910, the majority of newly built Veneklasen brick houses were within the city limits of Holland and Zeeland. It may have been rising prices that discouraged brick construction in the ru-

19. *Holland City News,* 15 January 1887. This figure is based on the cost of bricks used at the County Poor Farm in Eastmanville, in which 238,250 were sold for $1,460.49.

ral communities, but that was not the case among city dwellers, many of whom were profiting from booming industries. Here in the city, a peculiar development occurred in the style of the houses. These new city houses no longer featured patterned brickwork, and by about 1895 this craft had gone by the wayside. Perhaps those who were building in the city wanted a statelier, grander feel, in contrast to the small-scale, welcoming styles of the country houses. Some of the brick houses in the city, like the seven which comprised "Keppel's Village" on Central Ave. in Holland, were built for the middle class, but most were built for the wealthy.[20] These homes typically belonged to business owners, lawyers, or college professors. Many have well over 2500 square feet, stone slabs above and below their windows, a full basement, and two stories and a large attic. The brick on these houses is noticeably weaker than the brick from earlier periods. This may be due to diminishing supply of good clay. Yet because most of these houses lie within the respective historic districts of either Holland or Zeeland, they are mostly protected from development and are usually well kept.

20. For the construction of Keppel's Village see the *Ottawa County Times*, 3 August 1895, and 30 August 1902.

Chapter 3

Veneklasen Family and Business:
Prosperity and Troubled Times (1890-1930)

The family occupies a prominent position in the social circles
of the community, and is one of the foremost in the village.[1]

When Berend J. Veneklasen visited Holland in 1888, the *Holland City News* referred to him fully as "Mr. B. J. Veneklasen of the Groningen Brick Manufacturing Co."[2] The name of the company was ever-changing and the paper can be forgiven for its invented moniker. Regardless of the company's official name, it was the Veneklasen name itself that had become strongly associated with bricks and that guaranteed success. Never were there complaints of unfair business practices, and even when holding a near-monopoly, Veneklasen brick was sold at fair prices. The *Ottawa County Times* wrote, "Pluck, perseverance, and brains, combined with honest goods and upright dealing have made this great

1. *Portrait & Biographical Record*, 1893, 382.
2. *Holland City News*, 1 September 1888.

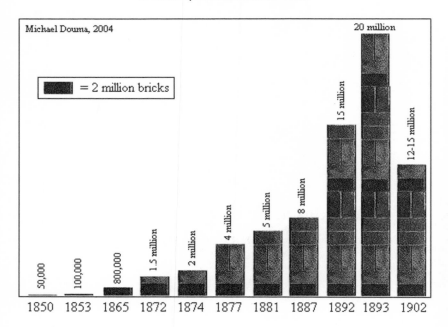

Michael Douma, 2004

= 2 million bricks

20 million

15 million

12-15 million

8 million

5 million

4 million

2 million

1.5 million

800,000

100,000

50,000

1850 1853 1865 1872 1874 1877 1881 1887 1892 1893 1902

Veneklasen & Co. / Zeeland Brick Co., yearly brick production, 1850–1902

business."[3] In addition, the Veneklasens kept up to date with technology. In 1890, when it was rumored that telephone lines would connect Zeeland, Overisel, and Fillmore, Veneklasen & Sons expressed a strong interest. In 1902 they added electric lights at their Zeeland yard. Of the Veneklasens' determination, the Holland City News wrote, "When they make up their mind to have anything, it is bound to come."[4] They also endeavored to use technology and new techniques to make better bricks. In the winter of 1910, Gerrit Veneklasen spent ten days at a brick maker's convention in Pittsburgh.[5]

With the successes of the brickyard, the Veneklasens were able to

3. *Ottawa County Times*, 30 December 1892.
4. *Holland City News*, 5 April 1890.
5. *Zeeland Record*, 18 February 1910.

Cloverdale Brickyard Factory, circa 1910, persons unidentified

also become involved in other types of business. They could be found as board members at some of the largest local companies, and were business partners with influential figures across the state. They also experimented with their own new business ventures, such as in 1886, when they planned to use their company's brick to build a shoe store in downtown Zeeland.[6]

In the last few decades of the nineteenth century, business at the brickyard continued to prosper, and brick production rose.[7] A fire at

6. *Holland City News,* 11 December 1886.

7. For figures on yearly brick production see *Ottawa County Times,* 22 August 1902., and *Holland City News,* 29 April 1876, 1 June 1878, 17 January 1880, 19 November 1881, 31 October 1891, 28 January 1888, and 16 January 1892.

the Zeeland yard in 1891 did little to halt the progress of the company. With no insurance (insurance was uncommon among the local Dutch in nineteenth century), the company had to cover the $1,200 damages out of pocket. Yet, the assets were on hand. The burned-down storage sheds were promptly rebuilt. The company also earned good press when a relieved Berend J. presented the Zeeland fire department with fifty dollars for their quick service in containing and putting out the brickyard fire.[8] Berend J. Veneklasen, who had started the brickyard with his father in 1849, stepped down from the business in 1892, leaving his $30,000 stock in the company to his children. Berend's eight sons, all of whom been working at the plant since youth, took over administrative duties. The company, which had heretofore been called Veneklasen & Sons, was incorporated under the name Zeeland Brick Company.

Under its new auspices, the Zeeland Brick Co. continued to prosper. And with success came expansion, making it for a time the largest business of its kind in the state. At its peak, the Zeeland Brick Co. may have accounted for up to 25% of the total brick production in Michigan. By 1893, Zeeland Brick Co. had two yards at Zeeland, one at Cloverdale in Barry County, and one in Hamilton.[9] From these yards they would expand further yet.

Successful brickmaking operations began in Cloverdale by 1876 and soon attracted others to the area. David Bates, an English immigrant, was the first to make bricks there and was followed up shortly afterward by George Hudson. On the numerous clay beds nestled between the glacial lakes common to the area, other attempts to found brickyards met varying success. Bates, as well as William Leonard who came to nearby Delton in 1908, each owned multiple yards. According to the 1905 report of the Bureau of Labor Statistics, the business owned by the Zeeland Brick Co. in Cloverdale was begun in 1888. This date probably refers to the year when the Bates brickyard became an officially registered business, the year following the introduc-

8. *Holland City News,* 31 October 1891.
9. Potrait & Biographical Record, 1893, 381-82.

tion of the railroad in Cloverdale. In 1892, Martin Bates had taken over the business from his father, David Bates. He now became associated with the Zeeland Brick Co. and even moved to Zeeland temporarily. It seems likely that Zeeland Brick Co. then provided capital to build a more substantial factory in Cloverdale in exchange for a commanding share of Bates' brickyard. Martin Bates continued on as the operator in Cloverdale, selling the yard, or his remaining share of it to the Zeeland Brick Co. in 1901, when he relocated to Kalamazoo. In Kalamazoo, Bates continued to work for the Zeeland Brick Co., operating yards for them in Kalamazoo along with the Cloverdale yard. Because a railroad provided a direct connection between these two locations, Bates could easily oversee both sites. Edward Pennels, a foreman at the Cloverdale brickyard for twenty years, also played an important role. He appears as a representative of the Zeeland Brick Co. in a 1903 financial ledger of William Leonard's Delton Brickyard (near Cloverdale).[10] The brickyard saw steady work and continued to thrive while the company expanded, taking ownership of and consolidating the resources of the local clay fields. In 1906, the Zeeland Brick Co. purchased the yard of Cloverdale's George Hudson. *Years Gone By*, a book which chronicles the history of Barry County, continues about the expansion of the Zeeland-owned yard in Cloverdale.

> [They] moved further East, locating their kiln back of the Evangelical Church. They operated on a bigger scale, employing more men and installing machinery to carry the clay up to the mixer. . . . A large deposit of clay enabled the company to continue this yard until 1914.[11]

When the Veneklasens gave up production in Cloverdale, Bates and Pennels continued to work the clay until it was exhausted. In 1915,

---

10. Delton Brickyard Ledger, 1897-1904, 7 and 305. Available at Bernard Historical Museum Archives.

11. Prosper G. Bernard, compiler, *Years Gone By* (Michigan: privately published, 1966), 185.

**Dettlof children with
excavated wagon, 2002**
Courtesy Denise Dettlof

the Zeeland Brick Co. gave left-over pallets from their defunct
Cloverdale yard to the brick company of William Leonard in Delton
in exchange for a horse that was to be delivered to their Hamilton
yard.[12]

The Veneklasens' yard in Hamilton was also quite substantial and
at times may have rivaled the output of the Zeeland yards. In 1890,
there were about forty men employed at Hamilton, where the company had two brick machines.[13] The yard was noted for producing a
superior sewer brick.[14] Unfortunately, documentation on the Hamilton yard is marginal at best. It is possible that Hamilton had an active brickyard as early as the mid-1860s when brick houses first appeared in southern Fillmore and Overisel townships, but there is no
evidence to support this. Hamilton's first serious brickyard enterprise was begun in 1883 by Pieter Oosting. In 1888, a Mr. Van Ark and
his son joined Oosting in ownership.[15] In turn, the entire brickyard

12. For information on Leonard Brickyard and Delton, Michigan, see the
website of Nancy Kroes at http://homepages.wmich.edu/~kroes/brickyard/.
13. *Holland City News,* 5 April 1890.
14. *Ottawa County Times,* 30 December 1892.
15. *Holland City News,* 19 May 1888.

was sold to Veneklasen & Sons in 1890. Albert Veneklasen relocated to Hamilton and took control of the yard. He and his immediate family lived in Hamilton for the better part of thirty years (1890-1920). Records of Hamilton Reformed Church show that both the families of Peter and Albert Veneklasen were in Hamilton in 1892, but by 1895, they had all left the church and were instead attending church in Zeeland.[16] Other family members came and went, living in Hamilton for a season or for a few years at a time, probably helping out with running the business. Jacob Hoeksema, a Holland native who first worked for four years with the Veneklasens in Zeeland, became the sub-manager of the Hamilton plant in 1892. In 1900, the "capable and trustworthy" Hoeksema took over as the manager in Hamilton.[17] Surprisingly, the only remnant of Hamilton brick in Hamilton itself is a brick house adjacent to the brickyard. In 2002, the residents of this house unearthed the metal frame of an old wagon, which they had discovered on their property two years earlier. The wheels and axles of this wagon are severely bowed, apparently from the stress of carrying bricks. When the wagon got stuck in the brickyard mud a century ago, it was simply left to waste away.

In 1899, the Veneklasens may have sought further expansion when a group of Zeelanders made an excursion to see the clay fields at Rudyard, Michigan, a town south of Sault St. Marie in Chippewa County.[18] In Rudyard, just a year beforehand, a Mr. Davidson had started a brickyard, and rumors of the extensive clay beds, some two hundred feet deep, spread. It appears, however, that the Veneklasens did not get involved in this area until 1920 and left soon thereafter.[19] Their involvement appears to have been strictly administrative.

By the twentieth century, Zeeland Brick Co. produced all sorts of materials in addition to bricks including drain tile and cinderblocks.

16. JAH Collection W90-1027.1, Church Members 1887-1892, p 13, and 1887-1942, p. 25.

17. Dr. Henry F. Thomas, editor. *A Twentieth Century History of Allegan County, Michigan* (1907), 385.

18. *Zeeland Record*, 26 May 1899.

19. Rudyard Centennial, *Recollections of Strongville* (2002), 9.

They dominated the West Michigan brick market, being one of only a few brick companies to have multiple yards. For a time the Veneklasens owned a yard in Kalamazoo, which may have been the source of brick for the new family home, a substantial 1910 remolding of the 1873 original. While the Kalamazoo brickyard is often referred to as one unit, it was really two distinct yards: Brownell (Alamo) and Oshtemo. This first Kalamazoo yard, called the Harris Farm brickyard, was located five miles to the northwest of Kalamazoo, and was purchased in the fall of 1900.[20] The Oshtemo, or second Veneklasen-owned yard, was sold to the Zeeland Brick Co. in 1906 by William Leonard, mentioned above in relation to Cloverdale and Delton.[21] Employment statistics show that in 1904, twenty-three men were employed at the first yard, but in 1905 the Zeeland Brick Co. was idle in the area. In 1906, Zeeland Brick Co. once again employed twenty men in Kalamazoo County, but this time at Oshtemo, their first brickyard (Alamo) having been completely consumed by fire the previous April.[22] Because the rest of Kalamazoo County has little clay, the city of Kalamazoo relied heavily on imports from brickyards in this area, which witnessed some of the earliest attempts at brickmaking in West Michigan. With some success, in no small part due to the railroad connections to Chicago, the Zeeland Brick Co. venture here lasted until 1914.

In 1903, the Zeeland Brick Co. expanded further still, buying the Collins Brickyard of Grand Rapids and reorganizing it as the Valley City Brick Company. The Collins brickyard may have been a gem in the eyes of the Veneklasen brothers for years, and it was only natural that they would acquire it. Located at the east end of Grand Rapids (between Fulton and Fountain Streets), the area known simply as "by the

20. More specifically this brickyard was located near the east end of the present-day Kal-Haven trail, along the Michigan Central Railroad, just east of US-131 and south of Twin Lake. Connections in this area may have been established through the wife of Roelof Veneklasen, Nellie Moerdyk, a Kalamazoo native. The 1910 Census lists Bernard Veneklasen as living in Kalamazoo.

21. Website of Nancy Kroes. http://homepages.wmich.edu/~kroes/brickyard/.

22. See chart entitled, "Zeeland Brick Co. Employment Statistics by Year and Location 1904-1919" in the following chapter. See also *De Grondwet*, 10 April 1906.

brickyard" was the most densely populated residential district in the city, peopled almost entirely by new immigrants from the province of Zeeland. A strong *Zeeuws* dialect could still be heard on the streets there well into the twentieth century. The brickyard community was poor and wages were low. Collins Brickyard along with the nearby Clark & Brown Brickyard and the earlier Simeon L. Baldwin Brickyard, among others, took advantage of these low wages and the vast clay deposits. The Veneklasen brothers planned to erect a new plant with a capacity of fifteen million bricks per year and the ability to run year-round.[23] Unfortunately, I have been unable to determine the fate of this brickyard. The lack of information may indicate that the brickyard was quickly resold, as the Valley Brick Co. ceased to exist after 1908.

It is not unlikely, given the size of the company and the entrepreneurial spirit of its owners, that the Zeeland Brick Co. would have been involved in brickyards in still more places. The *Holland City News* of 23 January 1903 mentions that the Veneklasens operated a successful brickyard in Muskegon. This may simply be a misprint or another short-lived and forgotten enterprise. With numerous worksites across the state, the business headquarters nevertheless remained in Zeeland throughout.

In 1904, tragedy struck when one of Berend's sons, Roelof (Ralph), died at only forty-eight years of age. The *Holland City News* claimed his was the largest funeral ever held in Zeeland. Hope College faculty and businessmen from all over West Michigan were present for the service. Even Holland City State Bank, of which Roelof had been a director, closed for the duration of the funeral. Roelof was widely known and respected. He had been director of the Holland Furniture Co., president of the Holland Sugar Co., and secretary and treasurer of the Zeeland Brick Co. He also had had interest in the above-mentioned Valley Brick Co. of Grand Rapids.[24]

---

23. *Holland City News*, 23 January 1903; *Evening Press* (*Grand Rapids Press*), 17 August 1901. See also Henry Ippel, "The Brickyard: A Dutch Neighborhood in Grand Rapids," *Origins*, Vol. 12, No. 1, 1994, 3-8.

24. *Holland City News*, 9 September 1904.

**Roelof Veneklasen, from portrait and biographical record of
Muskegon and Ottawa Counties, Michigan, 1893**

Roelof's connection to the brick business was deep-rooted, having begun working at the plant at only ten years of age and returned in various administrative capacities after attending Kalamazoo Business College. His expertise at the brickyard was surely missed.

The Zeeland Brick Co. was a family business through and through. The 1910 Ottawa County Census strongly illustrates this point, documenting that five Veneklasen brothers ran the company.

Peter Veneklasen, at 45 years of age, was the president, his brother Gerrit, 36, was the bookkeeper. Their brother John, 56, was the brickmaker, and his son John Jr. was a laborer at the yard. Henry, 49, and Albertus, 51, continued to work at the yard as they had done for decades. Bert Veneklasen, 29, was also at the yard full-time. Many other family members, especially the young men, may have worked part-time or seasonally. The six listed adult Veneklasen men, working full time at the yard in 1910, supported a total of at least twenty-two dependents. This included the widowed Minnie Veneklasen, who probably drew a paycheck from her late husband, Albert, who passed away in 1900.[25]

The wealth from a successful business allowed the Veneklasens to purchase what many others could not afford. For instance, in 1897, the *Zeeland Record* boasted of the shiny new bicycle of B. J. Veneklasen Jr., son of Roelof. Perhaps in a related story two weeks later, the same newspaper ran an article saying that many bicyclists, some of whom were "prominent citizens," had been breaking city ordinances by riding on the sidewalks. Others of the family traveled extensively: in 1897, Gerrit and Ben Veneklasen made a trip to Maine, while B. J. went to Texas with a friend, Albert LaHuis. In 1911, Gerrit, Ben, and John Jr. drove to Grand Haven, perhaps taking a ferry across Lake Michigan, where they sought repairs in Wisconsin for their "fine new touring car." This desire to travel seems to have stayed with the family throughout the early twentieth century. The family of John Jr. vacationed regularly in Florida, at a time when such vacations were rare. In the 1930s they even traveled by airplane.[26]

John Veneklasen Sr. passed away in 1920, his will showing him to be a wealthy man. He had had interest in most of the predominant local businesses. In addition to an automobile, he owned a store in

---

25. 1910 Ottawa County Census, part 1, pp. 116a, 116b, and part 2, pp. 235a, 235b, 239a, 250a.

26. *Zeeland Record*, 26 March 1897, 9 April 1897, 16 July 1897, 10 September 1897, and 3 March 1911.

John Veneklasen and family
Courtesy of Leslie Lampen

Zeeland; a farm in Heath Township, Allegan; and lots in Canada. In a middle school autobiography, Jane Veneklasen Lampen, the daughter of John Jr., wrote about growing up in the Veneklasen family in the 1920s. She recalls having had a pleasant childhood with frequent visits to Grand Rapids, piano lessons, a well-appointed room, and trips to Florida. About living in West Michigan in the summer she wrote, "I spend my summer months at my grandmother's cottage on Black Lake near Macatawa Park. . . . I surely have the summer vacations. Swimming, reading, riding, boating. Almost anything you wish to do whenever you wish to do it."[27] While other sides of the family may have had more practical matters to pursue and less free time, there is no indication that they struggled to get by.

The prosperity of the Veneklasens' Zeeland Brick Co. did not go unnoticed by other businessmen and other local brick companies were formed to compete. One example was the Holland Brick Co.,

27. Autobiography of Jane Veneklasen Lampen, private collection of Leslie Lampen.

which was founded in 1903 on the east side of Holland at the southwest corner of Fairbanks Avenue and 8th Street. Owned by real estate agent J. C. Post, this company took advantage of a sand hill near its plant to provide raw material.[28] Also in 1904, J. H. Nibbelink employed ten men in a brickmaking operation in Vriesland. Like the local brick manufacturers of the 1880's (Roost & Klaasen, Van den Beldt), these new brickyards met years of success but folded when hard times hit.[29]

By the turn of the century, the area's building boom was long past. Few houses were being built out of brick. The Zeeland Brick Co., although it reached its peak output in 1894, continued to prosper as it marketed its product for use in industrial and public buildings, where the stronger white bricks were well-suited. One particularly large order of bricks, roughly two million, was sent to the Kalamazoo Paper Co. in 1902.[30] Hope College, with which the Veneklasens had always had a strong relationship, also became an important customer, choosing to build with red brick. Hope College buildings from this period that were made of Veneklasen brick include Van Raalte Hall (1902) Voorhees Hall (1907), and Carnegie Hall (1906). As well, Veneklasen brick was supplied for the President's Home, which was built on the college's campus in stages from 1886 to 1892.

In the 1910s and 1920s, the volume at the plant dropped off considerably. At first, it was little cause for alarm. The Zeeland Brick Co., a fixture in the local economy, appeared to still be on solid footing in 1915 when it had a capital stock of $50,000. In 1916, the Veneklasens invested in five new kilns for their Hamilton yard.[31] They must have thought that the troubled times would pass and that demand would return. But, year after year the company was losing bids and losing money. Whether this was due primarily to low de-

28. *Ottawa County Times*, 28 December 1903, and 22 May 1903.
29. Holland Brick Co. ceased to exist around 1910.
30. *Ottawa County Times*, 22 August 1902.
31. *Hamilton Press*, 10 December 1954.

Zeeland Brick Company, Branch Yard, Hamilton, Michigan

mand, or low supply of remaining clay, or perhaps both, it is difficult to know; but in 1922 the Zeeland yard had openings for only fifteen to twenty workers. Sanborn Fire Insurance maps show that between 1916 and 1923 a large kiln shed at the Zeeland yard was torn down and not replaced. The main factory building had also been badly damaged from fire and wind.[32] In the summer of 1922 rumors circulated that the plant wasn't going to be operated at all that season. To avert this, Henry Veneklasen returned from Rudyard to manage operations in Zeeland.[33] Henry's brother Peter took over administrative duties up north, being noted as the manager of the Rudyard Brickyard in 1922.[34] The operating season of the Zeeland plant had diminished significantly. In the peak years of the 1880s and 1890s it was common for the plant to run from the first spring thaw to well into November, a season of up to thirty-five weeks.[35] In its last few years, operations at the brickyard ran for as little as three to four months.

32. Sanborn Fire Insurance Maps available at JAH Collection H88-0900, Reel 39, Zeeland Michigan, 1916, 1923.

33. *Holland City News*, 18 May 1922.

34. Jack Thornton, "Brick Making," in *Tales of Rudyard As Told By The Folks* compiled by J. W. Kitching (1922, repr. Rudyard Lions Club, 1973).

35. *Holland City News*, 19 November 1881.

Family of Berend J. Veneklasen, circa 1890
Courtesy of Leslie Lampen

A five-thousand-dollar fire at the drying sheds of the Hamilton yard added to Zeeland Brick Co.'s financial strain. Albert LaHuis, a Zeeland businessman and longtime friend of the Veneklasens, was hired to try to pull the company out of its financial difficulties.[36] In August of 1922, in a case before the U.S. district court in Grand Rapids, Zeeland Brick Co. asked to be declared bankrupt. The question was whether the assets of the company were worth more than its debts and liabilities. The *Zeeland Record* reported,

> If the petition of Ben, John H. and Bert J. [Veneklasen] goes through, 75 men working at the Hamilton and Zeeland plants will be out of work. The plants have already made millions of bricks this year. The Zeeland Plant has been idle for about one

36. *Holland City News,* 27 June 1922.

A Branch of the Veneklasen Family Tree

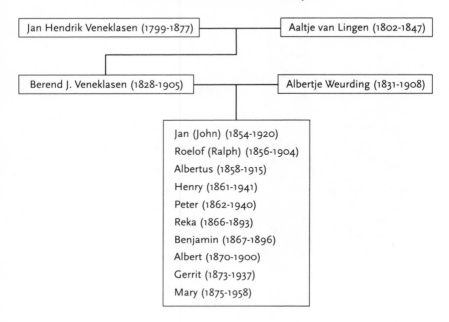

Jan Hendrik Veneklasen (1799-1877) — Aaltje van Lingen (1802-1847)

Berend J. Veneklasen (1828-1905) — Albertje Weurding (1831-1908)

Jan (John) (1854-1920)
Roelof (Ralph) (1856-1904)
Albertus (1858-1915)
Henry (1861-1941)
Peter (1862-1940)
Reka (1866-1893)
Benjamin (1867-1896)
Albert (1870-1900)
Gerrit (1873-1937)
Mary (1875-1958)

and a half years and needed considerable repair, but is now in full operation.[37]

The case must not have gone through initially because the yards continued production for the next two years. By March 1, 1923, work had begun at the Zeeland yard, but in Hamilton the yard didn't open until after April 5.[38] Perhaps the fire damage of the previous year had caused the Hamilton plant to open later. With all the financial difficulties, the Veneklasens were forced to cut wages of their laborers. In Hamilton, the workers saw a drop in pay of five cents per hour.[39]

After the deaths of Benjamin (1896) Albert (1900), Roelof (1904),

37. *Zeeland Record,* 17 August 1922.
38. *Holland City News,* 1 March 1923, and 5 April 1923.
39. *Holland City News,* 3 July 1924.

Zeeland Brick Company letterhead, printed in 1893 and still used in the 1920s
Courtesy Leslie Lampen

Albertus (1915), and John (1920), only three of Berend's eight sons remained: Henry, Peter, and Gerrit. These remaining brothers were nearing retirement age and may have felt that it was time to pull out of the industry. Peter, for one, found work elsewhere. In 1923, The *Zeeland Record* reported, "Peter Veneklasen, who has been employed at Zeeland Brick Co. at Rudyard, Michigan, the past years, and more recently Chicago, expects to move back to Zeeland in the near future. Mr. Veneklasen has accepted a position with the Holland Maid Manufacturing Co., at Holland."[40] As well, the younger generation of Veneklasens looked for its future away from the now-faltering family business. Henry's sons, Nelson (b. 1888) and Bernard (b. 1893) accepted positions with the road construction company of Plaggerman and Kimme. Bernard worked with a steam shovel, and Nelson served as a fireman.[41] James Veneklasen, Roelof's son, studied at Western Theological Seminary and went into ministry.

Although the yard was up and running in the spring of 1923, the Veneklasens were in talks to sell, and by June 14 the brickyard was purchased by a syndicate who planned on building a cold storage plant on the west Zeeland site.[42] In 1925, the Hamilton brickyard was sold off as well. The *Holland City News* noted, "The [Hamilton]

40. *Zeeland Record,* 15 March 1923.

41. *Zeeland Record,* 1 Mach 1923. Some of Zeeland's Veneklasens (James T., Joan, Paul S.) moved to California around this time.

42. *Holland City News,* 14 June 1923.

Right: Working at the Groningen or Zeeland yard, circa 1900
Courtesy Zeeland Historical Society

Below: Sketch of Zeeland Brick Company factory and Veneklasen family houses. According to legend, this sketch was made by a hobo.
Courtesy Zeeland Historical Society

Brickyard formerly owned by the Veneklasen interests has been sold to the Lincoln Brick company of Chicago, who are now operating the plant."[43] Any remaining interests of the Veneklasens in other brickyards around the state were likely sold at this time. John Veneklasen Jr., who in 1923 moved to Hamilton to run the plant there, returned to Zeeland in 1925. Bert Veneklasen, his brother, had already left Hamilton for Zeeland in 1922.[44] It appears that the remaining brothers were coming home for retirement.

43. *Holland City News*, 28 May 1925.
44. *Zeeland Record*, 27 July 1922. Also verified by Hamilton Reformed Church Records, JAH Collection W90-1027, Consistory Minutes, 18 December 1922.

The diminishing supply of suitable local clay for making bricks quite likely played a significant role in causing the end of the company. In 1934, the *Holland City News* blamed cement side walls and tile for replacing brick.[45] In one respect, the *News* may have been correct, but there were larger economic reasons for the downfall of the local brick industry. In the 1920's, many brickyards across the state declared for bankruptcy as the industry itself seemed to endure a period of restructuring. Contracts went to new companies, some from out of state, who had tapped into cheaper and more extensive sources of clay and who employed new technology. Transportation costs being minimized by railroads and trucks, the days of local brickyards were coming to an end.

45. *Holland City News,* 2 August 1934.

Chapter 4

Brickyards and Workers

With hundreds of workers employed locally in the industry at its peak in the late nineteenth century, brickmaking was an important provider of labor and a substantial contributor to the growth and wealth of West Michigan. The work was sometimes backbreaking, but the workers could take pride in seeing the fruit of their labor.

Brickmaking in the nineteenth century required both hard labor and skill. The first step in the process was to procure the raw material, namely clay. It was dug by hand, with pickaxes the tool of choice, and transported by horses or mules. Next, the clay was put into a grinder. Powered by horses in the earlier years but machine-driven later on, the grinder filtered out pieces of stone or pebbles in the clay; if pebbles were left in, the brick would be more prone to crack. Sand was also thrown into the mixture, providing strength. The machine grinder at the Zeeland yard was described as a "large machine with huge revolving knives which cut up and pulverize the clay."[1] After the clay was ground, it had to be shaped. At first the

---

1. *Ottawa County Times*, 30 December 1892.

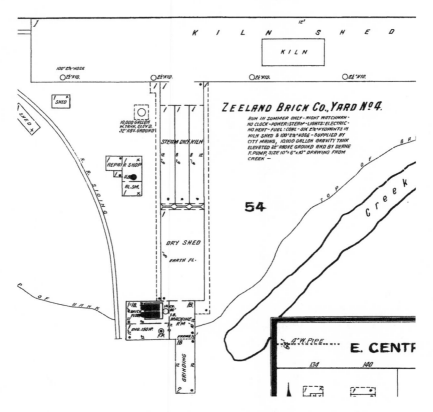

Sanborn Fire Insurance map of Zeeland Brick Company, 1908

clay was set by hand in wooden molds. In the 1870s, though, brick machines were introduced for this task. These machines would squeeze the clay out of a tube onto a conveyor belt and cut the bricks like sausages, creating highly uniform bricks. After being molded into shape, clay is traditionally known as 'green brick.'[2] Green brick

2. In Zeeland this clay was actually of a grayish color. Interview of Mrs. Henrietta Van Voorst by Barbara Dickman, 16 December 1976, available in Veneklasen file at Zeeland Museum Archives.

Zeeland Brick Company, Zeeland yard, date unknown
Courtesy Zeeland Historical Society

was left in the sun or in drying sheds for up to three weeks before being baked in large, high temperature kilns. In 1878 Veneklasen & Co.
burned 600,000 bricks in a single kiln.[3] A skilled brickmaker was
needed to make sure that the kiln was burning at the correct temperature — that is, between 950 and 1150 degrees Celsius.[4] Too much
heat or exposure would cause bricks to turn black or crack; too little
and they would be soft.

A brickyard (consisting of both a factory and several clay pits)
was not a forgiving environment. Coal and wood burning in the
kilns produced smoke and gave off excess heat in the already warm

3. *Holland City News,* 12 October 1878.
4. Campbell and Pryce, *Brick,* 30.

summer months. The grinding and cutting machinery in the factory produced noise overpowered only by the regular passing of trains. Proper equipment, such as leather gloves, offered the most protection — as did experience. With respect to accidents, the yard's uninitiated fared the worst. For instance, in 1881, a newcomer at Roost's yard in Holland was nearly killed when a clay bank caved in.[5] Fellow workers pulled out the stunned man, who was fortunate to walk away with nothing worse than bruises and a sore back. On 20 August 1901, the less fortunate Johannes Soer [also known as John Zoer] died from a similar accident at the Zeeland yard and was then buried in the nearby New Groningen Cemetery.[6] Experienced workers, including the Veneklasens themselves, were not immune to accidents. Sparks at the kiln blinded Henry Veneklasen, and Henry's son Bernard lost part of his hand in an accident at the yard. Entanglement in a brick machine could lead to a quick and gruesome death. To prevent such an accident, the Department of Labor in 1895 ordered the Zeeland factory to guard the main belt in its engine room.[7]

Perhaps more accidents actually occurred on the road near the Zeeland yard than at the yard itself. Here a large hill limited visibility and the road intersected with the railroad. At this spot in 1910 Bert Veneklasen flipped his car over into a ditch. Fortunately, he wasn't injured and the car suffered little damage. The local road commission frequently addressed the issue of poor road conditions at "brickyard hill" and there were many attempts at leveling the hill. But the intersection at the hill was still treacherous in 1924, when two motorists died there, their car being hit by the passing Interurban train.[8] Yet another road accident, this time not lethal, occurred at the same spot in 1929, when four boys lost control of their Ford sedan.

5. *Holland City News*, 29 May 1881.
6. *Holland City News*, 23 August 1901.
7. Annual Report of the Bureau of Labor Statistics [Michigan], with Appendix of Factory Inspections (1896), 145.
8. *Zeeland Record*, 10 June 1910 and 15 May 1924.

Workers at the Zeeland Brick Company's Cloverdale brickyard, circa 1910

The car somersaulted down an embankment on the brickyard hill and nearly landed in the creek.[9]

In 1887, the *Holland City News* reported that two brick masons were arrested for public drunkenness and thrown into the new brick jail. These lawbreakers didn't stay behind bars for long, though, as they were able to dig through the jail's brick wall and escape.[10] Indeed, across America brickworkers generally had a reputation as ruffians and drunkards. In West Michigan, though, such a reputation may have been undeserved. Apart from the rare instance of misconduct, the brickworkers in West Michigan appear to have been an acceptable crowd. Many brickyard employees and masons were married, adult men with families. The occasional secretary or other office worker excepted, women were never employed there. Children

9. *Holland City News*, 3 October 1929.
10. *Holland City News*, 15 October 1887.

under eighteen were not altogether uncommon at the site, but they remained a small minority of the workforce.

Working at a brickyard was demanding and exhausting. The yard would operate ten hours per day, six days a week (never on Sunday), and hours were sometimes irregular when bad weather interfered. But working at the brickyard had its advantages. In Zeeland, the Veneklasens provided their employees (at least for a time) with free lunch and dinner at the factory. Competitive wages at Veneklasen & Co. assured the workers a respectable standard of living. In 1881, workers' wages ranged from $1.10 to $1.40 per day.[11] But wages could fluctuate from season to season based on demand, and in some years brickworkers made little money. Fortunately for the workers, there was some wage competition with other brickyards. For instance, in 1874, John Roost was credited with paying his quarrymen the substantial sum of $1.50 per day.[12] Skilled masons, who were employed separately from the brickyards, earned even more and were unionized. In 1902, the masons and bricklayers in the Holland area announced that they would be charging forty-five cents per hour.[13] Meanwhile, the wages of brickworkers failed to keep up with those of other professions. The occupation became less desirable and brickyards were forced to hire immigrants and others who were desperate for work.

Labor department statistics from 1893 to 1919 illustrate the ebb and flow of employment at the brickyard in Zeeland. Employment peaked in the early 1890s, declined sharply, and then plateaued. The range of wages was probably affected by price of the bricks and the season's demand. In profitable years at the yard, employees benefited with higher wages, but poor years led to poor workers. Employment figures for all Zeeland Brick Co. yards, available from 1904 to 1919, are also revealing. While the Zeeland yard had regular work, demand for brick at other yards was less predictable. Most years without report indicate that the respective yard was idle or closed down.

11. Johannes Van Dyke in 1881 quoted in "The Holland Kolonie," 3-4.
12. *Holland City News*, 13 June 1874.
13. *Ottawa County Times*, 29 February 1902.

U.S. Dept of Labor Factory Inspection Reports
for Zeeland Brick Co., Zeeland yard, 1893-1901[14]

Year	Date of Inspection	Employment at Capacity	Employment at Inspection	Wages Per Day
1893	14 December		Idle	
1894	7 June	135	25	
1895	28 June	60	30	
1896	15 May	60	26	
1897		40	22	
1898		45	26	$1.31
1900		35	35	$0.99
1901	9 July	45	45	$1.60

Zeeland Brick Co. Employment Statistics
by Year and Location, 1904-1919

Year	Zeeland	Hamilton	Kalamazoo	Cloverdale	Valley City
1904	41	21	23	16	35
1905	47	19		16	26
1906	40	21	20	16	44
1907	36		20	15	33
1908	31		5	12	26
1909	41	19	9	3	
1910	42	19	24	16	
1911	36	17	27	12	
1912	31	21	3		
1913	25	21	25		
1914	21				
1915	21				
1916	14	15			
1917	21				
1918		25			
1919	24				

14. These charts are compiled from information found in Annual Reports of the Michigan Bureau of Labor Statistics and Appendices of Factory Inspections, 1893-1920. Presumably, the figures include both factory workers and field workers. The 1894 figures include the Groningen yard, which is not mentioned in other years, and may have been considered one and the same with the Zeeland yard.

Yntema house at 940 Paw Paw, built in 1894;
colored mortar creates a more solid color

It was uncommon for a brick company to own yards in more than one city, and rare for one to make more than one color of brick. According to a Veneklasen company letterhead printed in 1893, yards at Zeeland produced white brick, and yards in Hamilton made red brick. This has caused some previous researchers to assume that *all* red brick was from Hamilton, and *all* white brick was from Zeeland. The truth about the colors of Veneklasen brick is much more complicated. The Steketee House, built in 1851 a few miles outside of Zeeland, was made of reddish-orange brick; the source of the clay either in Holland or Groningen.[15] Later on in the Zeeland area, the Veneklasens still had one factory, but really two yards: Groningen

15. In the early 1850s imports of any kind were limited due to the lack of quality roads, and transporting red brick from outside would have been costly if not impossible.

Supply stack of red bricks at the Cloverdale brickyard

and Zeeland. The Groningen yards made red brick, while the Zeeland yard, which opened in 1872, made white. On the busy streets of Holland in 1883, it was reported, bricks were being shipped through the city to build a new house for a Mr. Mokma in Graafschap.[16] To ship bricks through Holland to Graafschap, the source must have been in Groningen or Zeeland, and the house of Mr. Mokma in Graafschap is not white, but red, demonstrating that the Groningen yard was still active and making red bricks. From 1872 to 1890, Veneklasen & Sons operated only these two yards, and only in Zeeland could someone load a wagon with both white and red brick. The majority of polychromatic brickwork houses were built in the 1870s and 1880s, and their red brick came primarily from

16. *Holland City News,* 20 January 1883.

**Ottawa County, poor house
(1887-1997)**
Photo © 1975, Zeeland
Historical Society

Groningen, not Hamilton. Despite significant red brick production at their Hamilton yard by the 1890s, and improved lanes of transportation, the Veneklasens in Zeeland continued to produce red bricks in addition to white. But the Groningen red brick evolved over the years into more of an orange-colored brick. This orange brick can be seen on such buildings as Voorhees Hall and the Western Michigan Furniture Building in Holland. After 1900, this solid orange brick became the brick of choice for city homes in Holland and Zeeland.

To summarize, I have identified a minimum of eight types of bricks produced at Veneklasen-owned yards, which include:

Holland Red — 1848-1852
Groningen Red — 1853-1890
Groningen Orange — 1890-1910
Zeeland White — 1872-1924
Kalamazoo Dark Red — 1900-1912 (multiple yards)
Hamilton Red/Orange — 1890-1925 (other owners 1865-1890)
Cloverdale Red — 1888-1914 (other owners and yards, 1876-1915)
Rudyard Brown — 1920-1923 (other owners 1898-1923)

The names of those who are responsible for the brickwork patterns are largely forgotten. On some houses the name of the builder has been inscribed in stone, but the builder did not usually design the brickwork. Credit for many of the designs goes to a Mr. Zuidam, who probably had apprentices and surely had imitators. Peter Oosting also constructed many Veneklasen houses and may have designed some brickwork patterns.[17] Oosting spent many years in the brick and concrete industry, and from 1883 to 1888, he even owned and operated the Hamilton brickyard, at that time a rival to Veneklasen & Sons. R. E. Werkman, a carpenter and owner of the Phoenix Planing Mill, is credited with carpentry projects for many brick houses and for the former County Poor House (also known as Community Haven) in Eastmanville, which also featured polychromatic brickwork.[18]

Architect James Huntley was also responsible for building with Veneklasen Brick. Huntley designed and worked primarily on large-scale building projects within the city of Holland. His Veneklasen brick buildings date to the 1880s and 1890s and include Hope Church, First Reformed Church, the 8th Street Fire Engine House, offices for West Michigan Furniture Company, and the President's Home at Hope College. Huntley preferred working with Groningen brick, and he never employed patterned brickwork. Instead, he used gray stone, often in archways, to contrast with the orange brick and form imposing facades.

17. P. Oosting is credited with construction of a schoolhouse in Holland Township and the Veneklasen houses of Keppel Village on Central Avenue in Holland. See *Holland City News*, 11 February 1882, and *Ottawa County Times*, 30 August 1902.

18. *Holland City News*, 24 July 1886. Werkman also built schools in Vriesland and Graafschap.

Part II

A Survey of Veneklasen Brick Houses

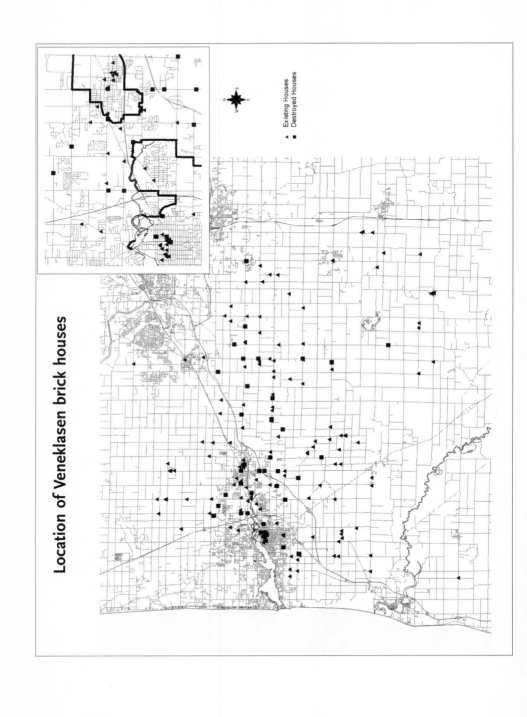

Location of Veneklasen brick houses

Existing Houses
Destroyed Houses

The next chapters will describe the location, architecture, and preservation status of Veneklasen brick houses. The above map of Veneklasen houses is based on the information gathered in a survey and found below in a chart. In the chart, houses are listed by county (Ottawa, Allegan, Kent), then sorted alphabetically by city or township, and finally sorted numerically by address. For the category 'brick color' I have simplified the colors of the bricks into red and white. The red color can also be many shades of orange, while the white brick has been referred to as being cream or buff color. To save space, polychromatic houses that are red with white bricks are listed as "RwW" for red with white. The same applies for "WwR" which stands for White with Red brick. "R+W" indicates that a house has an equal amount of both red and white brick. The year of construction is listed if known. The year of destruction is designated by the column "gone," and a "not applicable" or "n/a" means that the house is still standing. Finally, the last column "VH/BB" indicates whether the house was found by previous researchers, Van Hartesveldt in 1983, or Baron Bailey in 1998. Their earlier lists have been very helpful in compiling this expanded and updated list. This list and its resulting map are by no means complete. For instance, I have found only scant information on houses destroyed before 1980. As well, it is possible that some houses were simply missed during field work. If anything, there is a bias towards having too few houses, as I have included only the houses in which I can prove their existence through photographs or reliable historical sources. Also note that the resolution on the map is not perfect and if houses are in close proximity to each other, they may appear as only one house. A larger map can be seen at the Joint Archives of Holland.

Ottawa County

Location	Address	Brick Color	Built	Gone	VH/BB
Blendon	9194 Port Sheldon	RwW	1885	n/a	x
Georgetown	3594 Bauer	RwW	1874	n/a	
Holland City	8 E. 12th	Red	1889	n/a	
Holland City	11 W. 14th	Red	1890's	n/a	
Holland City	12 W. 13th	Red		n/a	
Holland City	18 E. 12th	Red	1894?	n/a	
Holland City	28 W. 32nd				
Holland City	30 E. 13th				
Holland City	36 W. 12th				x
Holland City	36 E. 12th	Red	1894?	n/a	
Holland City	39 W. 9th	WwR		n/a	x
Holland City	64 W. 64th	Red	1867,90		
Holland City	78 E. 12th	Red		1954	
Holland City	91 W. 10th			n/a	
Holland City	92 E. 10th	Red	1886-92	n/a	
Holland City	105 W. 12th	Red	1893-94	n/a	
Holland City	112 E. 12th			n/a	
Holland City	170 College	Red		1975	
Holland City	177 College	Red		n/a	
Holland City	188 W. 13th	Red		n/a	
Holland City	192 W. 12th	Red			
Holland City	236 9th	Red	1868	n/a	
Holland City	238 Washington	Red	1870	n/a	x
Holland City	241 Fairbanks	Red	1875	1961	
Holland City	268 Maple	Red	1902	n/a	
Holland City	284 Maple	Red	1883	n/a	
Holland City	318 Central	Red		n/a	
Holland City	324 Central	Red		n/a	
Holland City	330 Central	Red		n/a	
Holland City	334 Central	Red		n/a	
Holland City	350 E. 24th				
Holland City	378 W. 32nd	Red	1864	1993	
Holland City	751 Central	Red		n/a	
Holland City	827 Paw Paw	RwW		n/a	x
Holland City	883 Paw Paw	Red		n/a	
Holland City	940 Paw Paw	Red	1894	n/a	
Holland City	10362 Adams	Red		n/a	
Holland City	40th + Washington	Red		1980's	
Holland City	(unknown) 8th St.	WwR			

Holland City	(unknown, Schaap)	RwW			
Holland City	unknown-VanGoor	Red		Yes	
Holl. Twp.	264 96th			1983-98	x
Holl. Twp.	376 N. Franklin	RwW	1887	n/a	x
Holl. Twp.	398 120th				
Holl. Twp.	473 120th				x
Holl. Twp.	1046 96th			1983-98	x
Holl. Twp.	1448 96th	WwR	1870?	1983-98	x
Holl. Twp.	1811 112th	Red	1851	n/a	
Holl. Twp.	2499 Beeline				x
Holl. Twp.	2791 104th	Red	1866		
Holl. Twp.	2896 128th				
Holl. Twp.	3797? Beeline	RwW			
Holl. Twp.	3810 Beeline	RwW		n/a	x
Holl. Twp.	3990 112th	WwR	1850's?		x
Holl. Twp.	4155 120th	RwW		n/a	x
Holl. Twp.	9699 Ottogan	RwW	1870	n/a	x
Holl. Twp.	9793 Ottogan				x
Holl. Twp.	10244 Perry	RwW		n/a	x
Holl. Twp.	10441 Mason			1983-98	x
Holl. Twp.	10537 Paw Paw	WwR	1882	n/a	
Holl. Twp.	10720 James	RwW	1885	n/a	x
Holl. Twp.	10715 Paw Paw	RwW	1857	2003	x
Holl. Twp.	10967 Riley			1983-98	x
Holl. Twp.	11045 Paw Paw	RwW	1859, 85	n/a	x
Holl. Twp.	11593 Greenly			1983-98	x
Holl. Twp.	11771 E.Lakewood	RwW	1860?		
Holl. Twp.	11952 James				
Jamestown	215 Riley	RwW		n/a	x
Jamestown	291 44th				x
Jamestown	595 24th	RwW	1880		
Jamestown	955 32nd	WwR		n/a	x
Jamestown	1060 Perry	RwW		n/a	x
Jamestown	1095 Riley	RwW		n/a	x
Jamestown	1385 Byron	RwW	1866	1998	
Jamestown	1389 Perry			yes	
Jamestown	1630 32nd	RwW		1950	
Jamestown	1754 Perry	RwW		n/a	x
Jamestown	2294 Byron	RwW	1889	n/a	x
Jamestown	2323 8th			n/a	
Jamestown	2337 Byron				x
Jamestown	2400? Adams	WwR			
Jamestown	2465 32nd	WwR			

Jamestown	2995? 24th	WwR		1919	
Jamestown	3420 Adams	RwW	1866	n/a	
Jamestown	3426 Perry	White	1874	n/a	
Jamestown	3530 8th				x
Jamestown	3559 Perry	Red		n/a	
Jamestown	3690 Byron	Red	1897	n/a	
Jamestown	3735 Adams				x
Jamestown	3950 40th (same as parsonage?)	WwR		1983-98	x
Jamestown	4265 Adams				x
Jamestown	5587 School Ave.	WwR		n/a	x
Jamestown	Unknown- Forest Grove School	RwW	1885?		
Olive Twp.	5321 112th				
Olive Twp.	6091 96th	RwW	1880	n/a	x
Olive Twp.	6231 96th				x
Olive Twp.	6297 96th	RwW	1888		x
Olive Twp.	6448 112th				x
Olive Twp.	6500 112th				x
Olive Twp.	6834 120th				x
Olive Twp.	6934 112th				x
Olive Twp.	12878 Van Buren	RwW			x
Zeeland City	4 E. Main	Red		1975	
Zeeland City	37 N. State	WwR	1882	n/a	x
Zeeland City	37 E. Main (Museum)	WwR	1876	n/a	x
Zeeland City	59 Maple		1885	n/a	x
Zeeland City	119 S. Maple				
Zeeland City	120 S. Church	Red	1872	n/a	
Zeeland City	149 S. Maple				
Zeeland City	214 E. Central	Red	1899	n/a	
Zeeland City	225 E. Washington	RwW			x
Zeeland City	227 E. Washington	WwR			x
Zeeland City	336 E. Central	RwW	1885	n/a	x
Zeeland City	338 E. Lincoln	RwW	1880's?	n/a	x
Zeeland City	501? W. Main	RwW	1870	1961	
Zeeland City	644 E. Central	RwW	1889		x
Zeeland City	10219 Chicago Dr.	RwW		1970's	
Zeeland City	10231 Chicago Dr.	White	1880's	n/a	
Zeeland City	10263 Chicago Dr.	White	1880's	1985	
Zeeland City	10271 Chicago Dr.	WwR	1873?	n/a	
Zeeland City	10283 Chicago Dr.	Red	1873, 1910	n/a	
Zeeland Twp	170 72nd			1983-98	x
Zeeland Twp.	449 76th				
Zeeland Twp.	2215 48th				
Zeeland Twp.	2450? 64th	RwW	1878		

Location	Address	Brick Color	Built	Gone	VH/BB
Zeeland Twp.	3074 80th	RwW			x
Zeeland Twp.	3655 56th	RwW			x
Zeeland Twp.	3741 64th	RwW	1867	n/a	x
Zeeland Twp.	4181 88th	RwW			x
Zeeland Twp.	4265 Adams				
Zeeland Twp.	4570 80th		1860?		
Zeeland Twp.	5245 Adams	WwR			x
Zeeland Twp.	5445 Adams	RwW		1977	x
Zeeland Twp.	5860 Byron				x
Zeeland Twp.	5970 Adams	Red		n/a	
Zeeland Twp.	6154 Adams	WwR	1873	n/a	x
Zeeland Twp.	6645 Adams	RwW		1996	
Zeeland Twp.	6701 Adams			1983-98	x
Zeeland Twp.	6747 Adams	RwW		n/a	x
Zeeland Twp.	6881 Byron	RwW	1878?	n/a	x
Zeeland Twp.	7300? Byron	RwW		Yes	
Zeeland Twp.	8015 Quincy	WwR	1893	n/a	
Zeeland Twp.	8475 Adams				
Zeeland Twp.	8770 Adams				
Zeeland Twp	(unknown) Adams?	RwW	1886		
Zeeland Twp.	(unknown) Beaverdam	WwR			
Zeeland Twp.	(unknown) Drenthe School	RwW		yes	

Allegan County

Location	Address	Brick Color	Built	Gone	VH/BB
Dorr Twp. (school)	1395 138th	Red	1908	n/a	
Dorr Twp.	1853 136th	RwW	1873	n/a	
Dorr Twp.	3670 14th			n/a	
Dorr Twp.	3819 14th			n/a	
Dorr Twp. (school)	4219 18th			n/a	
FillmoreTwp.	1067 Graafschap				
FillmoreTwp.	A1305 Russcher				x
FillmoreTwp.	A4041 Blue Star	Red			
FillmoreTwp.	3968 52nd	RwW		1950	
FillmoreTwp.	4051 60th				
FillmoreTwp.	4305 49th			1983-98	x
FillmoreTwp.	4781 52nd			1983-98	x
FillmoreTwp.	4782 52nd	RwW		1995-98	x
FillmoreTwp.	5065 146th	RwW		1995?	
FillmoreTwp.	5092 140th				

FillmoreTwp.	5185 140th	RwW		n/a	x
FillmoreTwp.	5185 Russcher	RwW		n/a	
FillmoreTwp.	5207 141st				x
FillTwp. (school)	5615 138th				
FillmoreTwp.	5736 140th	R+W	1872	n/a	
FillmoreTwp.	5958 Church				
FillmoreTwp.	5984 Church				
FillmoreTwp.	5988 Church	Red	1880's	n/a	
FillmoreTwp.	5992 141st				x
FillmoreTwp.	Russcher School	RwW			
Heath Twp.	3282 M-40	Red		n/a	
Heath Twp.	3320? M-40	Red		1990	
Hopkins Twp.	216 Elm			n/a	x
Hopkins Twp.	220 Main			n/a	x
Hopkins Twp.	322 Maple			n/a	
Hopkins Twp.	425 Maple			n/a	x
Hopkins Twp.	1614 130th			n/a	
Hopkins Twp.	1624 135th			n/a	
LaketwnTwp.	6187 147th	RwW		n/a	
LaketwnTwp.	6215 146th	Red	1881	n/a	
LaketwnTwp.	6300 147th	Red	1885	n/a	
Manlius Twp.	4938 136th	Red		n/a	
Manlius Twp.	5014 136th	Red		n/a	
Manlius Twp.	5946 136th	RwW		n/a	x
MontereyTwp	2612 130th			n/a	
MontereyTwp	2645 130th			n/a	
MontereyTwp	(school) 3391 130th				
MontereyTwp	3215 128th	Red		n/a	
MontereyTwp	3408 30th			1983-98	x
Overisel Twp.	3814 44th	RwW		n/a	x
Overisel Twp.	3841 44th	RwW		1973	
Overisel Twp.	3977 43rd				x
Overisel Twp.	3984 43rd				x
Overisel Twp.	4029 47th	Red	1878	n/a	
Overisel Twp.	4046 43rd				
Overisel Twp.	4071 45th	RwW		n/a	
Overisel Twp.	4088 47th	Red		n/a	
Overisel Twp.	4109 142nd	RwW		n/a	x
Overisel Twp.	4160 142nd	RwW		n/a	x
Overisel Twp.	4283 142nd	RwW		1950	
Overisel Twp.	4382 140th	RwW		n/a	
Overisel Twp.	4425 44th	Red		n/a	
Overisel Twp.	4426 142nd				x

Overisel Twp.	4488 46th	RwW			
Overisel Twp.	4493 144th	Red		n/a	
Overisel Twp.	4549 145th				x
Overisel Twp.	4581 145th	RwW	1878		
Overisel Twp.	(school) 4595 143rd	RwW	1885	1958	
Overisel Twp.	UnknownParsonage	RwW	1880	1927	
Salem Twp.	2985 146th				x
Salem Twp.	3213 146th	RwW		n/a	x
Salem Twp.	3260 142nd			1983-98	x
Salem Twp.	3267 142nd			2001	
Salem Twp.	3339 146th			1983-98	x
Salem Twp.	3365 142nd	WwR		n/a	x
Salem Twp.	3373 146th	WwR		n/a	
Salem Twp.	3553 146th				x
Salem Twp.	4420 32nd				x
Saugatuck Twp.	6214 136th				
SaugatuckTwp.	(school) 6295 124th	RwW	1898-99	n/a	

Kent County

Location	Address	Brick Color	Built	Gone	VH/BB
Byron Twp.	2455 Prescott	RwW		1990's	x
Byron Twp.	2471 146th	White		n/a	
Byron Twp.	2899 92nd	RwW		n/a	x
Byron Twp.	4151 108th			n/a	
Byron Twp.	9352 Homerich			n/a	x
Byron Twp.	9832 Ivanrest	Red		n/a	
Byron Twp.	10245 Ivanrest	RwW	1904	n/a	
ByrTwp-school	84th +Homerich	RwW	1891	n/a	
Byron Twp.	100th? + Ivanrest?	RwW	1904		

Chapter 5

Location and Distribution
of Veneklasen Houses

A survey of Veneklasen brick houses conducted throughout the summer of 2004 had the goal of documenting the history and architecture of as many Veneklasen houses as possible. It soon became obvious that it would be much more manageable to create spatial boundaries and limit the search accordingly. The area chosen for the survey thus included: the two bottom rows of townships in Ottawa County (Park, Olive, Holland, Zeeland, Laketown, Georgetown, Jamestown); the two upper rows of townships in Allegan County (Laketown, Fillmore, Overisel, Salem, Dorr, Manlius, Heath, Monterey, and Hopkins); and Byron Township in Kent County. This selected area represents the whole of the Dutch immigration to Holland, Michigan, and its environs. Although many nineteenth-century Dutch emigrated to Grand Rapids, Muskegon, and Kalamazoo, these cities have not been included. While Veneklasen bricks were sent in large quantities to those cities for constructing industrial, commercial, and public buildings, I have seen no evidence of their use in a residential setting.

The question invariably comes up: "Just how many Veneklasen

**Large farmhouse of John Kleinheksel at 3968 52nd Street
in Fillmore Township, destroyed 1950**
Photo courtesy of Ruth Tidd

houses are there?" This question is difficult to answer. What exactly qualifies as a Veneklasen house? If we consider the number of houses that were primarily made of brick from one of the many yards owned by the Veneklasens, the number of houses must be well over three hundred. The question that seems more appropriate is "How many Veneklasen houses are there that have patterned brickwork?" This number is still surprisingly high, at over one hundred. Many individuals may be surprised at these figures. Some residents of these houses believed that there were no more than fifty such houses in total. Veneklasen houses are most commonly seen along what were the main thoroughfares of the period of their construction. These houses were built to be seen and they are on hilltops, where they can overlook the countryside. Yet other brick houses were built in fairly remote areas, seen only by those who live near them. It is interesting to note that the distribution of houses roughly represents population patterns of the period. For instance, Blendon Township, which was only sparsely populated in the nineteenth century, has only a few representative brick houses. The city of Hudsonville, a relative latecomer in the area, didn't have a post office until 1872, and only has one remaining Veneklasen brick house. Saugatuck never built with brick because it was connected to the lumber industry and it was spared by the great fire of 1871.

Certainly there are many Veneklasen brick houses which stand outside the surveyed area. The city of Allegan, for one, has a high density of Veneklasen homes. In 1884, the city of Allegan burned down and was thereafter rebuilt largely with Hamilton brick. With a direct rail line from Hamilton to Allegan, bricks could be shipped in large numbers. There may be more than twenty Veneklasen houses remaining in downtown Allegan, as well as another twenty public buildings and churches. Only a few of these have polychromatic brickwork. Additionally, the cities of Otsego and Plainwell feature Hamilton brick. A similar survey project and further study needs to be conducted to learn about Veneklasen homes in Allegan city as well as central and southern Allegan County.

An unnerving dilemma for the survey lies in not knowing which local brick houses were made from brick from other brickyards. It is possible, if not likely, that some of the surveyed brick houses in Allegan County were created with Hamilton brick during the tenure of another manufacturer, as the Veneklasens did not purchase the Hamilton yard until 1890. In Overisel Township, a few houses may have been built from bricks procured on site, as was the house at 2323 8th Street in Jamestown Township. These houses have been included, but this self-production of bricks was rare, and no more than a handful of remaining houses belong to this category. It is also possible that a few houses from the 1880s in Holland may have been made with brick from the yard of Roost & Klaasen. For instance, the red bricks of the house at 751 Central Avenue in Holland are of a darker shade than most Veneklasen houses. On the Eastern edge of the survey there are a few contemporary nineteenth century houses made of white/yellow brick from another source, possibly in Byron Center or Burlingame. These houses have not been included. What appears certain is that all local houses with polychromatic brickwork were made primarily of Veneklasen brick. It is also worth noting that in Barry County, on the road from Hamilton to Cloverdale, one finds Veneklasen houses made of Hamilton brick and dating to around the turn of the century.[1]

Homes built of clay from the Zeeland Brick Co.'s yard in Cloverdale should also be included as Veneklasen houses. In Cloverdale itself there are six houses, two stores, a town hall, and a schoolhouse that were all made from this local clay during the years of Veneklasen ownership (1888-1914) of the brickyard.[2] In the township there are over thirty brick houses dating to this period. However some of the houses were built with brick from private brickmakers or from the nearby Leonard Brick Co. in Delton. Cloverdale witnessed substantial production and must have exported the majority of its bricks. Bricks were shipped along the Chicago Kalamazoo & Saginaw railroad which conveniently ran along the edge of the yard. Although the railroad was never extended to Saginaw, as it name indicates, it did continue past Hastings to Woodbury, Michigan. The main market for Cloverdale brick may have been Chicago. Across the tracks from the brickyard is a spring-fed lake, whose waters provided ice for the Chicago market. Also near the clay fields is a sand hill, sand being a necessary ingredient in making brick. Cloverdale clay has a very similar color (dark orange/ red) and texture to the Hamilton clay. This may have something to do with common techniques or mixtures that the Veneklasens used at their brickyards. A new house at the old Cloverdale site has been built upon a hill of brick rubble, discarded fragments (bats) of failed, over-baked kilns. The foundation of the Cloverdale factory is still visible. Veneklasen

1. Two of these houses are 688 Pierce Road near the town of Doster, and 10463 Norris Road in Prairieville.

2. Bernard, *Years Gone By*, 185.

houses are also found to the north and to the east of the surveyed area. Specifically, I have located these houses near Allendale. Zeeland Brick was used for businesses in Musekgon — one example being the large factory of C. L. King & Co. built in 1891 — and may have been used for houses as well.[3] In Montague, Zeeland white brick was used for the stately 1874 Franklin House Hotel and a neighboring residence.

Veneklasen houses, or more likely yet, schoolhouses, might very well be found in most counties in the western half of Michigan's Lower Peninsula. In 1892, the *Ottawa County Times* even wrote of Veneklasen brick being shipped to Indiana and Illinois.[4] The polychromatic, patterned brickwork styles, passed on by the Dutch in West Michigan, may be imitated in even more distant places. I have heard rumors of a similar style of houses in Ontario, Canada, en route to Toronto. Could it be coincidence that the will of John Veneklasen, who died in 1920, indicates that he owned lots in Sandwich and Essex, Ontario?[5] While this is intriguing, it may be misleading. The brickwork in Ontario may instead find its roots in an English style.

Within the surveyed area there was some confusion and misinterpretation about the origin of the brickwork houses. Particularly in Byron and Dorr Townships, there exists a belief that local patterned brickwork houses were made by the Pennsylvania Dutch (Germans).[6] According to one conversant, a group of nomadic Pennsylvania Dutch carpenters spent a decade in the area building houses before moving elsewhere. Just exactly how and why the Pennsylvania Dutch would have come to West Michigan is perplexing. I cannot say that there is no truth behind this myth whatsoever, but it fails to

3. Veneklasen brick was also used to build the Muskegon Opera House in 1878. *Holland City News*, 9 February 1878.

4. *Ottawa County Times*, 30 December 1892.

5. Copy of the will of John Veneklasen is available at JAH collection H04-1540.5.

6. For an example of this myth see the *Grand Rapids Press Southwest*, December 8, 1981.

Methodist church in Hopkins, Michigan

account for the large number of patterned brick houses built over a span of more than twenty-five years. Ultimately, this myth likely stems from an inability of many Americans to distinguish between Dutch and German, as well as a knowledge that Germans have created patterned brickwork elsewhere in America.

Through contact with non-Dutch communities, the Dutch craftsmen may have passed on patterned brickworking techniques, but the patterns never became as popular outside the Dutch-American communities. In the Polish emigrant community of Hilliards, Michigan, there stands a church built out of Veneklasen red brick with white brick inlay. While the arches of this church are round with patterned brickwork, other architectural lines of the church are sharp and triangular. Near the church is a Veneklasen brick home which may date to 1873. In Hopkins, Michigan, there are three Veneklasen houses and a church. The church is built on a traditional Methodist plan and features pointed arches. Brickwork crosses run in a pattern under the roofline.

Chapter 6

Architecture and Construction

Here and there, especially in Drenthe and Overijssel [Overisel] one sees sizable brick homes. Those are no longer farm houses, but manors built of red brick. They are five windows in width, four windows in depth, and two stories high.[1]

J. P., 1880s

From an architectural standpoint, the Veneklasen brick houses of West Michigan are unique. They exhibit a mixture of styles and influences from across the Netherlands in conjunction with popular trends in home design in nineteenth century America, all the while utilizing vernacular materials for construction.

Some brick houses, such as the former Van Raalte homestead on Fairbanks Avenue, were lived in for years as wooden houses and were only later encapsulated with brick. Many brick houses could somewhat more accurately be labeled 'brick-veneer' houses because

1. Jacob Van Hinte, *Netherlanders in America,* 337.

Brickwork pattern under roofline at 3810 Beeline Road

their frames are built of wood. I have measured some of these wooden support beams at 8 × 12 inches. On a few houses that have had porches removed, smaller wooden beams can be seen projecting out of the brickwork. Only after the wooden frame was complete could the brick masons begin their work on the exterior. The exterior brickwork is notable for its consistency. Mortar between the bricks was used conservatively and the bricks were laid in a uniform fashion.

These houses, with their solid construction, warmth in the wintertime and coolness in the summer months, deserved a look as pleasing as their feel. The distinguishing look of Veneklasen brick houses is their Dutch-influenced patterned brickwork. Brickwork patterns range from very simple arches that contrast with their surrounding brick, to intricate designs found under the roof line. In regards to the window arches, Van Hartesveldt noted six traditional

Patterned brickwork window arch at 3990 112th

designs, all variations on using alternate colors and half or full bricks in rows of soldiers (a soldier is a vertical-standing brick).[2]

Some brickwork patterns may have religious meanings as well as aesthetic appeal. Crosses are commonly found within the patterns, and it is possible that these crosses are indicative of the Protestant faith of the masons or their patrons, but nothing has been found to validate this conjecture. The unique brickwork pattern at 10244 Perry may represent a chalice or a beacon, both common religious symbols. Another feature of Dutch architectural influence is the use of metal ties. Found on nearly every *herenhuis* (lord's house) in Amsterdam and many *boerenhuizen* (farmers' houses) in the Dutch

2. Van Hartesveldt, "Patterned Brick," 35.

**Right: 10244 Perry in
Holland Township**

**Below: Kooyer's home at 378
32nd Street in Holland,
demolished in 1993**

countryside, these metal ties have a structural as well as a decorative
purpose. A metal tie is bound to the wall through the cement layers
between the bricks. It compresses the bricks and provides support to
the wall. Metal ties are often used to spell out the date of the building's construction. The Kooyers House, built in 1864 and destroyed
in 1993, provides an example of this. Perhaps because of their ex-

pense, metal ties were uncommon on Veneklasen homes. My survey
has located only about a dozen examples.

While a few architectural features are undeniably Dutch in origin,
others derive from contemporary America styles of the period. Examples of this conformity to American styles are the floor plans of
Veneklasen houses (prior to additions), which are mostly L-shaped
or T-shaped, although some are shaped as boxes.[3] The larger section
of a house is typically around 28 x 28 feet, while a second section, if
there is one, may be smaller at about 20 x 20 feet. At least one of the
two sections of the house is two stories tall. By the 1890s, these
homes had become more elaborate. While early houses typically had
six to seven rooms, later ones could have as many as ten or eleven.
Unlike in the Netherlands, these houses were never attached to a
barn. The roofs are generally less steep than those in the Netherlands
or in Dutch New York, and many have six or more surfaces. Also of
American influence are the slender, Italianate windows. In their original state, most Veneklasen houses had at least two fireplaces and a
stove in the center of the home that burned both wood and coal.

---

3. At least one Veneklasen house is octagon-shaped, a style which was common
across America in the 1850s and 1860s, when many octagonal houses were used as
stops on the Underground Railroad.

These houses also contrast with Dutch colonial houses in New York, which often have long, sloping roofs, are built of stone, and have characteristic features like a *stoep* and a Dutch door (a door split at mid-level).

Most Veneklasen houses have "Michigan basements." These basements, known now for their relatively short ceilings and cramped passageways, were altogether foreign to the Dutch immigrants. In the Netherlands, one would perhaps have only a small *kelder* (cellar) for storing food, not an open space running under the entire house. Because the Dutch were unfamiliar with basements, as such, they readily added the English word 'basement' to their vocabularies.[4] Basements in nineteenth century West Michigan were important for storing food items like potatoes, as well as for coal, oftentimes kept in a separate coal room. Additionally, basements often had cisterns were water could be stored for washing clothes. This water could be well water or run-off rainwater. Elongated metal windmills provided power to pump the water to the basement cistern. Because these cisterns were built below ground the water rarely froze in the winter.

In the basements one can take a look at the foundations of the houses, which can be used, in part, to help date brick houses. The earliest Veneklasen brick houses, such as the 1851 Steketee House, have foundations of brick. By the 1860's, fieldstone became a popular substitute for brick, which often proved too porous to protect from water seepage. Improved fieldstone foundations consist of hewn rocks, often of various colors, held together with mortar. These foundations, sometimes up to twenty inches thick, are structurally strong and typically show little wear from weathering. The dense, grey, Waverly stone was also used in foundations. While the Waverly Quarry was operating on the east side of Holland as early as 1866, it wasn't until 1885, when a Mr. F. Bird bought the quarry and organized the Waverly Stone Company, that this fairly expensive stone

---

4. Jo Daan, *Ik was te bissie...: Nederlanders en Hun Taal in de Verenigde Staten* (Barchem, The Netherlands, Walburg Press, 1987), 58.

This unique octagon-shaped house at 595 24th Street in Jamestown has been drastically altered since this photo, circa 1900

was popularly used for local foundations.[5] Waverly is more commonly found in city houses than country houses. A few buildings in Holland, including Graves Hall on the campus of Hope College, and the Clock Tower on Eighth Street, are made almost entirely out of Waverly stone.

Veneklasen brick was also used for carriage houses. Few of these survive today. These carriage houses likely met their fate when automobiles replaced horse-drawn transportation. Other outbuildings,

5. *Holland City News*, 14 May 1887.

including outhouses, were made of wood. Two curious examples of outbuildings of Veneklasen houses are (1) an ice storage shed at 940 Paw Paw Drive, and (2) a milkhouse at 6881 Byron Road. Large wooden barns, some original examples, typically compliment the country houses. These barns commonly feature the same fieldstone foundations as the houses. There appears to be no general rule for the layout of a farmstead, and barns can be found to any direction of a house. The houses, however, were built on hills whenever possible. While this is a generally intelligent thing to do, it might also reflect an inherited desire of the Dutch to protect against flooding.

The nineteenth-century housing market, it must be remembered, was much different than today's. Houses weren't built by large companies and then put up for sale to make a profit. Most houses were designed specifically for their buyers, who had purchased land and now wanted to build a home. Because these houses were individually tailored, designed, and constructed by various people, each one is unique.[6]

6. The only exception is Keppel's Village in Holland, where seven houses were built on the same plan.

Another view of the octagon-shaped house at 595 24th Street

Chapter 7

Future of the Houses and Conservation

Many people have expressed frustration and sadness at witnessing the gradual transformation of their once-distinctive communities into bland, formless, suburban agglomerations of subdivisions and shopping centers.

Randall Arendt, *Rural by Design*

In general, this quote seems to summarize the feelings of many homeowners that I visited while conducting this survey. Historic houses, if they do not draw tourist dollars, are difficult to preserve and protect. Since 1983, no fewer than twenty-five Veneklasen brick houses in the Holland area have been destroyed. For many owners of local nineteenth-century brick houses, there are strong pressures to sell their land to developers; brick houses in the countryside especially face a considerable threat. Between 1992 and 1997 alone, 5,678 acres of farmland in Ottawa County and 9,467 in Allegan County were consumed by development.[1] If the present rate of suburban

1. *Holland Sentinel,* 28 March 2004.

Veneklasen house at 4 East Main in Zeeland, Michigan, destroyed 1975
Courtesy of Leslie Lampen

growth continues and half-hearted attitudes towards preservation persist, these brick houses will be decimated within the next quarter century. A few houses that I have visited have already been slated for destruction. The growth of an industrial area around Tulip City Airport to the South of Holland threatens the brick house at 64 West 64th Street. While this expansion is legitimate and in many cases necessary, it cannot continue unchecked. It is not productive to try to save all historic structures by halting economic progress, but they must also not be tossed aside along the way and be destroyed so quietly.

For many historic houses, their respective passings-away have hardly been noted; others receive a short newspaper article. One such example was the Veneklasen house at 4 East Main Street in

Zeeland, which was razed in 1975. The *Zeeland Record,* a local paper with limited circulation lamented,

> Another one of Zeeland's finest old homes came tumbling down this week when the Veneklasen home on the corner of State and Main gave way to the wrecker's hammer. This home was erected in the era when refinement superseded speed and ease of construction. This was one of the most elegant homes built with Zeeland brick around the turn of the century.[2]

Some houses have come down only after their owners put up a valiant protest. In 1998, Dean and Pat Hoezee-Meyer, residents of Jamestown Township, purchased a Veneklasen house at 1385 Byron Road, intending to save the structure from developers and renovate it. This house, described as a "mansion" was well-worn, and had been used for migrant housing for some time. While early estimates put the cost of relocating the house at $23,000, the heart-breaking truth was that it would cost over $200,000 to move the crumbling brick structure. The Hoezee-Meyer's salvaged everything they could (doors, windows) from the house and then allowed the Jamestown Fire Department to burn down the remaining frame.[3] Some of the bricks were then put to use as another Jamestown family with a Veneklasen house purchased the bricks to build a matching garage.

This wasn't the first time that a Veneklasen house had been burned down on purpose. In 1996, a brick house at 6645 Adams Street was set ablaze by Zeeland Township which used the burning house for a training exercise for their Fire Department.[4] The house had been unoccupied for years and was falling apart. Short of a massive renovation, it could not have been saved. Once again the owners managed to salvage some of the bricks to create a fireplace for a new house on the same property.

2. *Zeeland Record,* 12 June 1975.
3. *Grand Rapids Press* Lakeshore Edition, 27 April 1998, 22 October 1998.
4. *Holland Sentinel,* 30 April 1996.

Main entrance to Quincy Elementary School in Zeeland, 2004

Historic houses are inherently difficult to protect because they are usually owned by private individuals. Preservation, then, needs to be a priority of local governments. The City of Zeeland, perhaps more than any other local governing body, is conscious of its past and much has been done to continue the architectural tradition of its nineteenth-century settlers. For perhaps the first time in over a hundred years, Dutch patterned brickwork reminiscent of the Veneklasen houses will be employed locally.[5] Both a new school and a new hospital will soon feature red brick similar in color and texture to the Veneklasen brick.[6] The new elementary school at 10155

5. In the near past, brickwork in the Veneklasen (or Neo-Veneklasen) style has been used on the building at 53 W. 8th St. in Holland. As well, a brick fire house, taken from Grand Rapids, was re-assembled in this style in Allendale.

6. *Holland Sentinel,* 10 March 2004 and 22 April 2003.

Quincy in Zeeland even features brickwork patterns reflecting those of local houses. GMB Architect Loren "Bud" Lothschutz found the patterns welcoming to the children and pleasing to the eye. With encouragement of Marcia Wirth, the principal at Cityside Middle School in Zeeland and board approval, Mr. Lothschutz began plans for the school. To match the color and texture of Veneklasen bricks, the new bricks, purchased from Robinson Brick Co. in Colorado, were 'tumbled' in a ready-mix maker. This gave the bricks a rough, nineteenth century look. The school opened in the fall of 2004 and is a credit to all those involved.

Preservation of Veneklasen brick must also be an issue on Main Street in Zeeland and 8th Street in Holland, both of which have received awards for their retention of historic architecture. I estimate that one third to one half of the buildings of these respective downtown shopping districts are made from Veneklasen brick. Some of these buildings have been refaced, plastered, or thoroughly renovated, therefore making provenance difficult to trace. Veneklasen brick buildings may date to as late as 1928, considering that surpluses of brick might have been available for a few years after the company's demise. It appears that the vast majority of surviving pre-1928 buildings on Main Street in Zeeland are of comprised of Veneklasen brick from the company's Zeeland and Groningen yards. In Holland, however, this is a different story. In addition to Veneklasen brick from Groningen, Zeeland, and Hamilton, Holland's downtown may feature bricks from the 1880s Roost & Klaasen brickyard, the turn-of-the-century Holland Brick Co., or imported bricks from other manufacturers. Because these downtown areas are well-established and thriving, preservation seems to be fairly certain for the time being.

Because historic districts and downtowns are fairly secure, local preservation efforts should be focused on Veneklasen houses in the countryside. But how can we save the Veneklasen houses of West Michigan? In 1998, Janna (Baron) Bailey suggested three ideas for preservation and conservation: a self-guided driving tour, a preservation organization, and the development of a Veneklasen house into a museum. I will explore these ideas and offer still others.

A self-guided driving tour is very possible but faces some challenges. Tulip Time visitors could be encouraged to not only drive down "Tulip Lane" through Holland, but also travel the countryside to see these houses. A pamphlet could be made to be distributed at the Chamber of Commerce. Still, it is difficult to predict what the level of interest would be, on behalf of both the homeowners and the visitors. This tour would require the permission of the owners of the involved houses. After having personally spoken with many of the owners, it appears to me that there is suitable interest in such a project. Tourists would not necessarily be led through the houses, but only look at them from the road. Owners of houses included in the tour would be motivated to keep up the appearance of their houses, and could possibly be compensated by Tulip Time Incorporated, which directs all Tulip Time activities.

A specialized preservation organization also seems to be a possibility. There has been much positive response from those who have taken part in this summer survey. Combined and organized, they could form a strong voice for study and preservation. This could be an outreach program of a local historical society. An annual meeting would be sufficient to discuss developments of the last year, address the threats that certain houses face, and plan for events like Tulip Time.

The development of a Veneklasen-style house into a museum has also been rumored. This would provide an income for a house, perhaps create a historic status, and save the house from developments. With the expansion and growth in West Michigan, a museum even in the farmlands of Ottawa County would have many potential visitors within a close driving radius. Such a museum could also teach city children about life on a nineteenth-century farm. The largest obstacle for the creation of a museum would be acquiring funds. Perhaps the Holland Museum, which overseas the Cappon House, the Settlers House, and the Ben Van Raalte House, would be interested in acquiring a brick house, given the right price and tax incentives.

The best way to protect an individual Veneklasen brick house is through the care of its owners. I have been deeply impressed by some

Abandoned house at 215 Riley in Jamestown Township, 2004

owners who have spent thousands of dollars and hundreds of hours repairing brickwork or restoring a room to its original condition. As long as there is interest in purchasing "fixer-up" projects and owning unique, historic houses, I see a long future for Veneklasen homes. Perhaps someday soon these houses will earn the respect they deserve, and we will honor the hard work and skill of the nineteenth-century Dutch craftsmen who built them, as well as recognize the place of Veneklasen brick houses in the history of the Dutch in West Michigan.

Bibliography

Books

Arendt, Randall. *Rural by Design: Maintaining Small Town Character.* Chicago: Planners Press, American Planning Association, 1994.

Bernard, Propser G., compiler. *Years Gone By.* Privately Printed, 1966. Available at Bernard Historical Museum.

Campbell, James, and Will Pryce. *Brick: A World History.* London: Thames and Hudson, 2003.

Daan, Jo. *Ik was te bissie . . . : Nederlanders en Hun Taal in de Verenigde Staten.* Barchem, The Netherlands: Walburg Press, 1987.

Galema, Annemieke. *Van de Ene en de Andere Kant: Noordnederlandse en Noordwestduitse migratie naar de Verenigde Staten in de negentiende eeuw.* Groningen, The Netherlands: Rijksuniversiteit Groningen, 1993.

Harger, Swenna, et. al. *Aus der Grafschaft Bentheim in die Neue Welt: 1640-2002 Geschichten und Daten von Auswanderern und ihren Nachkomen.* Nordhorn, Germany: A. Hellendoorn KG, 2002.

Lane, Kit., project director. *The History of Allegan County.* Dallas, Texas: Curtis Media Corporation, 1988.

Bibliography

Light, Sally. *House Histories: A Guide to Tracing the Genealogy of Your Home.* Second edition. Spencertown, N.Y.: Golden Hill Press, 2000..

Lucas, Henry S. *Dutch Immigrant Memoirs and Related Writings.* Grand Rapids: William B. Eerdmans Publishing Co, 1955, reprinted 1997.

McAlester, Virginia and Lee. *A Field Guide to American Houses.* New York: Alfred Knopf, 1984.

Meeske, Harrison Frederick. *The Hudson Valley Dutch and Their Houses,* Fleischmans, N.Y.: Purple Mountain Press, 1998.

The Overisel Colony: The First 150 Years. The Overisel Sesquicentennial Committee, 1998.

Portrait & Biographical Record of Muskegon & Ottawa Counties, Michigan. Chicago: Biographical Publishing Co., 1893.

Reynolds, Helen Wilkinson. *Dutch Houses in the Hudson Valley before 1776.* New York: Dover Publications Inc., 1965.

Stott, Annette. *Holland Mania: The Unknown Dutch Period in American Art and Culture.* Woodstock, N.Y.: The Overlook Press, 1998.

Thomas, Dr. Henry F., editor. *A Twentieth Century History of Allegan County, Michigan.* 1907.

Van Hinte, Jacob. *Netherlanders in America.* Translated by Adrian de Wit and edited by Robert P. Swierenga. Grand Rapids: Baker Book House, 1928, reprinted 1985.

Articles

Doucet, Michael J., and John Weaver. "Material Culture and the North American House: The Era of the Common Man, 1870-1920." *The Journal of American History,* Vol. 72, No. 3 (December 1985), 560-587.

Ippel, Henry. "The Brickyard: A Dutch Neighborhood in Grand Rapids." *Origins,* Vol. 12, No. 1, 1994, 3-8.

Kroes, Florence Leonard. "A History of Brickmaking," 1966. And assorted articles and writings from website of Nancy Kroes available at http://homepages.wmich.edu/~kroes/brickyard/. Copies of articles available at Joint Archives of Holland.

Marek, Don. "It's What's Under the Roof That Counts." *Grand Rapids Press Wonderland Magazine,* 21 September 1975.

Thornton, Jack. "Brick Making." In *Tales of Rudyard As Told By The Folks.* Compiled by J. W. Kitching. 1922. Reprinted by the Rudyard Lions Club, 1973.

Van Dyke, Johannes. "The Holland Kolonie." *Origins,* Vol. 1. Number 2, 1983.

Van Hartesveldt, Fred. "Decorative Brick: A Gift to Michigan From the Dutch." *Michigan History,* May/June 1987, 33-37.

Vande Water, Randy. "Veneklasen Brick." *Holland Historical Trust Review,* Vol. 3, Number 6, 1991.

Thesis

Bailey, Janna (Baron). Unpublished Master's Thesis on Polychromatic Brick Buildings in Ottawa, Allegan, and Kent Counties. Eastern Michigan University, 1998.

Newspapers

(IN DUTCH)

De Hollander
De Verzamelaar
De Grondwet
Sheboygan Nieuwsbode

(IN ENGLISH)

Holland City News
Ottawa County Times
Holland Sentinel
Grand Rapids Press

Booklets

"Sites of Dutch Influence in Western Michigan," Dutch-American Historical Commission, 1996.

"Dekker Huis Zeeland Historical Museum Presents: 2004 Tour of Homes & Churches." Zeeland Historical Museum, 2004.

Index

Index

Index